M000105870

Behind the Mask

of Religious Traditions

Your Guide to Discovering and
Destroying Sacred Cows

BEHIND THE MASK

OF RELIGIOUS TRADITIONS

Your Guide to Discovering and
Destroying Sacred Cows

by
Mark Briggs

© Copyright 2006—Mark Briggs

All rights reserved. This book is protected by the copyright laws of the United States of America. This book may not be copied or reprinted for commercial gain or profit. The use of short quotations or occasional page copying for personal or group study is permitted and encouraged. Permission will be granted upon request. Unless otherwise identified, Scripture quotations are from the King James Version (KJV). Scripture quotations marked (TM) are taken from THE MESSAGE. Copyright © 1993, 1994, 1995, 1996, 2000, 2002. Used by permission of NavPress Publishing Group. Scripture quotations marked (NIV) are taken from the HOLY BIBLE, NEW INTERNATIONAL VERSION. Copyright © 1973, 1978, 1984 by International Bible Society. Used by permission of Zondervan Publishing House. All rights reserved. Emphasis within Scripture quotations is the author's own. Please note that Destiny Image's publishing style capitalizes certain pronouns in Scripture that refer to the Father, Son, and Holy Spirit, and may differ from some publishers' styles. Take note that the name satan and related names are not capitalized. We choose not to acknowledge him, even to the point of violating grammatical rules.

Destiny Image® Publishers, Inc.

P.O. Box 310
Shippensburg, PA 17257-0310

"Speaking to the Purposes of God for this Generation
and for the Generations to Come."

For Worldwide Distribution, Printed in the U.S.A.

ISBN 10: 0-7684-2401-1

ISBN 13: 978-0-7684-2401-0

This book and all other Destiny Image, Revival Press, MercyPlace, Fresh Bread, Destiny Image Fiction, and Treasure House books are available at Christian bookstores and distributors worldwide.

For a U.S. bookstore nearest you, call
1-800-722-6774.

For more information on foreign distributors, call
717-532-3040.

Or reach us on the Internet:
www.destinyimage.com

1 2 3 4 5 6 7 8 9 10 11 / 09 08 07 06

Dedication

To my wife of nearly 30 years, Laquita, who has been patient and trusting through more than one major transition. She has believed in me even at times when my own believing was a little weak.

Acknowledgments

No man's work stands alone. An idea is born and then the real work begins in nurturing and converting the concept into the tangible. Special thanks go to the people who dedicated themselves to the entire process of what you now see and touch.

I thank God for my family—Laquita, Marcus, Marla, and Mandi; for Riverpark Church; Tom Winters; Debby Boyd; Wendy Hinds; Frances Attaway; Grady Brown; Pam Nolde; Sandy Varnell; Don Milam; Joel Nori; and Dean Drawbaugh.

Endorsements

Mark Briggs serves us a heap of meaty ribs in his book on "sacred cows." He's quite creative as he takes us on a journey that "ain't no crooked trail." And his "prime rib of truth," based on God's Word, will make a meal for your entire family—and your local family of faith.

—Dr. Dennis "The Swan" Swanberg
America's "Minister of Encouragement,"
TV host, author, humorist, and entertainer

In this book, Mark Briggs strips away the religious rituals and brings our focus back to a relationship of intimacy with God.

—John Bevere
Author, speaker
Messenger International
USA/Australia/United Kingdom

Warning! Read with care! This book will rip off your mask.

Some of us have worn religious masks for such a long time that we no longer know how to divide between religious tradition and the true Gospel of Christ. We have become comfortable hiding behind the disguise of our denominational heritage and personal theologies that are nothing more than "sacred cows."

—Gary McSpadden
Oakridge Boys,
Bill Gaither Trio and Vocal Band, The Imperials
Gospel Music Hall of Fame

Mark Briggs calls us to remember that there is a difference between culture and Christianity, and that we must continually discern which is which. He points us back to the only true standard—the Word of God—and reminds us that Christ is our perfect example.

—Twila Paris
Christian songwriter and recording artist

Behind the Mask of Religious Traditions is truly eye opening. If we are ever going to make a difference in this world for Jesus Christ, then we are going to have to realize what is behind the masks in our lives. Pastor Briggs has done a marvelous job of not only revealing some of the secrets behind the masks but also providing a godly plan for us to effectively deal with what we see.

—Hollis Conway
Two-time Olympic medalist
Author and evangelist

Real Christianity is the cry of Pastor Mark Briggs. This book is a powerful, "no holds barred" look behind the masks of Christian religion and straight into the heart of a God who desires relationship with us.

This book is destined to become a standard for those who are leaving the bondage of mere religion for the pursuit of authentic Christianity.

—Dr. Phil Brassfield
President, Destiny Vision Center, Inc.

Table of Contents

Introduction

ONLY three quick steps away from my car I ascended onto a stone-clad walkway that cut and curved its way through a plush carpet of emerald green grass. Mixed with the fresh smell of blooming flowers was the lingering scent of an earlier spring shower—sort of that clean and fresh aroma. In the distance I could hear the sound of music. From the immaculate parking lot to the polished handrail, everything said, "This is the place to be." I knew tonight would be a special treat. I guess that's why my steps quickened as I approached the massive carved oak doors bearing a sign that read, "Welcome."

With eagerness I grasped the brass handle of the huge right door, quietly easing it open so as not to disturb the activity inside. To my surprise, I couldn't see anything; something just inside the door was blocking my view. I opened the left door—the same result. If I couldn't *see* inside, how in the world was I going to *get* inside? Once more I opened the door and peeked in, this time making more of an effort to assess the situation. What I discovered was disconcerting to say the least. Two ushers built like bodyguards were stationed at the back of the church with their backs nearly touching the entry.

I couldn't get past them regardless of how desperately I wanted to. The people who were supposed to be helping me were actually blocking my entry! I'm sure to the people inside felt that these strategically-placed sentinels brought a certain sense of comfort and security; but I was not inside and could not gain access without causing some disturbance—defeating my whole purpose.

A pastor very seldom has an opportunity to slide into a church service unnoticed and simply be a worshiper. Very few people inside, if any, would recognize me, considering how far I had traveled from my hometown. I not only wanted to be here but I needed to be here—to blend into the worship, to be challenged and blessed by the message.

With a little effort and a whole lot of grace—God's grace, that is—I eventually made it past the sentinels and found a seat among the "well seasoned saints." I halfway expected to see a bright light and hear a deep baritone (God voice) say, "Well done, thou good and faithful servant. In spite of the opposition from inside you made it through the doors. Congratulations!" (Matt. 25:23 emphasis added).

After all this work I was determined now more than ever to get a blessing from the evening. I received more than I asked for. Along with the blessing came a few lessons I hadn't expected.

One of the main lessons I learned: the church looks totally different from the outside looking in than it does from the inside looking out. We add splash to our church world with words that sound ideal and affectionate, then we drown them with heartless actions. The church I visited said "Welcome" but it actually was not welcoming at all.

The only way we can fix this type of problems is to change, starting from the inside and working out. Sometimes changing is no more than just trying out our own front door. We get too accustomed to the garage entry and forget that guests come through the front. As silly as it may sound, occasionally I need to visit me at my house.

As a third-generation pastor, I have personally witnessed numerous major and minor changes in the "religious world"— some for the good and many more from bad to worse. My ministry travels have allowed me to view and visit numerous "the way we do it" camps in various denominations, governments, countries, and cultures. Some have been truly impressive, and some not so.

The one major difference between the successful and the super-successful is the ability to adapt and adopt. Successful groups tend to adapt in order to follow a trend. The super-successful will adopt new ideas and create a trend.

Adaptation adjusting our system to fit the changes around us when we are forced to do so. *Adoption* is making a conscious decision to change prior to our environment. In other words, instead of being changed we become the agency of change. Adaptation is prone to be passive. Adoption is prone to be active. Adaptation makes us followers. Adoption enables us to be leaders. If we choose not to adapt to the changes around us and never adopt new ideas within us, the organization dies.

When I say an organization dies, it's not as simple as it sounds. A tremendous amount of time can lapse between the death and the awareness of that death state. From the outside looking in, the entity being observed has every appearance of life and energy. Don't be deceived. It is only serving as host to some microorganism that is attracted to emptiness. Like the hermit crab that animates a vacated seashell, a religious system and its subculture can simulate true spiritual activity.

This simulation is the nature of the beast. When the real ceases to function as it should, this colossal animal of old ideas, icons, and traditions automatically takes over. I call it a "cow" which eventually becomes a "sacred cow."

This large beast, and whatever mask it may wear, consequently gets more attention and praise than the real cause it was originally created to serve.

As I expose my heart over the next few pages, I want to thank you for allowing me to share some food for thought. I feel very confident, whether you agree totally with me or not, that you will most definitely be challenged to change, once you see what is behind the masks.

I feel the need to warn you about making extreme radical changes. Don't go so fast and far that the peers around you and the followers behind you can't find you.

Out of obligation, I should also warn you: There is never a need to "throw the baby out with the bath water." The truth is, if the baby grows up, it will throw out its own bath water!

What you are about to read are reflections of an ex-rancher (so to speak) who used to build fences and guard the corral. As you absorb each word, please take time to glance between the lines. Listen and feel the heartbeat of a simple shepherd who understands the benefits of a fold and the potential dangers of a fence. The word *fold* itself denotes the ability to bend, flex and change, while the word *fence* represents rigidity, regulation, and incarceration. I'm not advising you to tear down your fences, but rather to convert them to folds.

Jesus spent major portions of His time on earth ripping off the masks of established religion. He was constantly folding and bending lines of *exclusion* into circles of *inclusion*—making room for "whosoever will." Jesus has always been and will forever be "out of the box" because He's into "the circle." Through Christ, God bent Himself into the circle of humanity allowing us access to the sphere of divinity.

I invite you to walk with me behind the masks of religious traditions, to see the ridiculousness of the religious box, and to step into the light and life of the Jesus circle.

Epigraph

And when God is personally present, a living Spirit, that old, constricting legislation is recognized as obsolete. We're free of it! All of us! Nothing between us and God, our faces shining with the brightness of His face. And so we are transfigured much like the Messiah, our lives gradually becoming brighter and more beautiful as God enters our lives and we become like him.

*Since God has so generously let us in on what he is doing, we're not about to throw up our hands and walk off the job just because we run into occasional hard times. **We refuse to wear masks and play games. We don't maneuver and manipulate behind the scenes.** And we don't twist God's Word to suit ourselves. Rather, we keep everything we do and say out in the open, the whole truth on display, so that those who want to can see and judge for themselves in the presence of God (2 Corinthians 3:17–4:2 TM).*

God hath given you one face and you make yourselves another.

—*William Shakespeare, Hamlet*

CHAPTER 1

Cows That Create
Crooked Trails

"Drinking From Muddy Ruts or From Still Water"

No doubt, you've heard the old saying "till the cows come home." Well, they have not only come home...massive herds have stampeded through the Kingdom, destroying some of the most truly sacred and precious principles our Father has instructed us to practice. They have become sacred cows, masters of masquerade.

They disguise themselves in steeples, seats, and sanctuaries; clerical robes, community programs; and even church worship services. They are not exclusive to tangibles, but may be seen on any given day of the week and in random events, ceremonial processes, methods of dress, or styles of music. The label usually reads: "Holy," "Righteous," or "Sacred"; yet they only resemble a residue of something they used to be. These sacred cows are no more than deified devices that may have worked at one time but have long since been trodden under hoof. This doesn't mean they are altogether bad, but they are never always good either. We have been guilty of creating "life-long loves" out of what should have been "limited editions."

There are many things in life that the Bible has little or nothing to say about. There are also things that God, in His infinite wisdom, saw fit to remain silent about. Sacred cows are not one of them.

Words of Wisdom

My four-year-old crawled up in my lap one evening as I was leisurely reading my Bible. The pages were open to one of the few places in the Gospel of John where there was very little *red letter* to the edition. After a very long period of silence, which is so uncharacteristic of a four year old, she looked up at me and asked, "What's the red letters for?"

I said, "Oh baby, that's where Jesus is talking."

After an even longer period of silence, she replied, "Hmm, He sure didn't have much to say."

After I finished chuckling, I explained to her that even when Christ's words were weak in number, they were always loud in volume.

The words my little girl spoke that day have resonated in my spirit numerous times since. So much so that I have sincerely asked myself, "What issues *did* Christ talk about?" And if He talked about them, they must have been of utmost importance.

With just a glance at the ministry of Christ, you can quickly see one of His main focal points during His three and one-half years of ministry on earth was the destruction of systems and anything that displaces the King of the Kingdom.

One day on the beaches of Gennesaret, the people in the area decided to gather all those who were sick to touch the edge of Jesus' clothing, *"and whoever touched him was healed"*(Matt. 14:36 TM).

This simple action seemed to offend the Pharisees, so they started criticizing: *"Why do your disciples play fast and loose with the rules?"* (Matt. 15:2 TM)

Jesus put it right back in their laps, saying, *"Why do you use your rules to play fast and loose with God's commands?"* (Matt.15:3 TM)

He went on to tell them what fakes they were, then He quoted Isaiah and said they were teaching what sounded good to them and using God for a cover. The disciples came to Him later and told Him the Pharisees were *really* offended now!

The Bible says, *"Jesus shrugged it off. 'Every tree that wasn't planted by my Father in heaven will be pulled up by its roots. Forget them. They are blind men leading blind men. When a blind man leads a blind man, they both end up in the ditch'"* (Matt.15:13-14 TM).

In other words, anything that cannot trace its genetics back to the Father will not be allowed to live. The end result of following blind leaders is blindness, which causes us to deviate from the main path and into the ditch.

Ditch People

In today's world there seems to be an entire community of what I call "ditch people." They are all tattered, torn, mangled, and muddy. Their entire emotional being is frayed and fatigued as a result of their struggle to come out of the ditch. There was never a thought of ending up here. They were traveling a road they thought was righteous, following leaders they thought had vision—only to discover the leaders were nearsighted and the road of righteousness had merged with the thoroughfare of religion.

The statement of purpose of the Lamb of God is *"to seek and to save the lost"* (Luke 19:10 NIV). The sad part is that we are becoming more and more difficult to be saved, as we have gradually blended into the religious herd and are sometimes buried beneath the defecation of our beloved bovines.

A stark reality: there are millions of people starving in India and yet there are millions of "sacred" cows they refuse to kill for food. We criticize their ignorance, all the while protecting our own unendangered species. There are people in our cities and communities, and, yes, sitting in our pews who are spiritually starving, but they cannot get to the Cross because of the cows. They need the Savior, but all they can see is the system. They seek a Messiah but are frightened by a man-made mask that has little or no resemblance to a redeemer.

I'll admit that religion provides a morsel for the hungry, but the starving are only made sick by the miniscule. The energy they spend while searching for the table often exceeds the nutrients provided by the meal.

The Mission

As the Holy Spirit leads us through the remainder of the book, our mission will be to rip away the numerous masks of religious traditions, and then search and destroy anything that resembles these cloven-footed cud-chewers. Many will die a slow and painful death, but they will die; because in the Father's green pastures cows and sheep cannot graze together.

Cows are contented with muddy ruts, but sheep passionately crave "still water."

On crooked trails silent lambs run the risk of falling into ruts of religion designed exclusively for the burial of the deceased. Perhaps it's about time we discover real direction, not from a righteous rancher, but directly from our Chief Shepherd. The Shepherd's passion is to provide numerous "still water" adventures to prevent us from walking down a calf-path created by the complacent.

"The Calf-Path"

One day, through the primeval wood,
A calf walked home as good calves should;
But made a trail all bent askew,
A crooked trail as all calves do.

Since then two hundred years have fled,
And I infer the calf is dead.
But still left behind his trail,
And thereby hangs my moral tale.

The trail was taken up next day
By a lone dog that passed that way;
And then a wise bell-wether sheep
Pursued the trail o'er vale and steep,
And drew the flock behind him, too,
As good bell-wethers always do.

And from that day, o'er hill and glade,
Through those old woods a path was made;
And many men wound in and out,
And dodged, and turned, and bent about
And uttered words of righteous wrath
Because 'twas such a crooked path.
But still they followed—do—not laugh—
The first migrations of that calf,
And through this winding wood-way stalked,
Because he wobbled when he walked.

This forest path became a lane,
That bent, and turned and turned again;
This crooked lane became a road,
Where many a poor horse with his load
Toiled on beneath the burning sun,
And traveled some three miles in one.
And thus a century and a half
They trod the footsteps of the calf

The years passed on in swiftness fleet,
The road became a village street;
And this, before men were aware,
A city's crowded thoroughfare;
And soon the central street was this
Of a renowned metropolis
And men two centuries and a half
Trod in the footsteps of that calf.

Each day a hundred thousand rout
Followed the zigzag calf about;

And o'er this crooked journey went
The traffic of a continent.
A hundred thousand men were led
By one calf near three centuries dead.
They followed still his crooked way,
And lost one hundred years a day;
For thus such reverence is lent
To well-established precedent.

A moral lesson this might teach,
Were I ordained and called to preach:
For men are prone to go it blind
Along the calf-paths of the mind,
And work away from sun to sun
To do what other men have done.
They follow in the beaten track,
And out and in, and forth and back,
And still their devious course pursue,
To keep the path that others do.

But how the wise old wood-gods laugh,
Who saw the first primeval calf!
Ah! Many things this tale might teach—
But I am not ordained to preach.[1]

Endnote

1. Sam Walter Foss, *Poems That Live Forever* (Doubleday, 1965).

Epigraph

Strangely, the expounders of many of the great new ideas of history were frequently considered on the lunatic fringe for some or all of their lives. If one stands up and is counted, from time to time one may get knocked down. But remember this: a man flattened by an opponent can get up again. A man flattened by conformity stays down for good.

—*Thomas J. Watson, Jr.*

A journey of a thousand miles begins with a single step.

—*Lao-Tzu*

Once harm has been done, even a fool understands it.

—*Homer*

Notes

_____

_____

_____

_____

_____

_____

_____

_____

_____

_____

_____

_____

_____

_____

_____

_____

_____

_____

_____

_____

_____

_____

CHAPTER 2

Cows That Are Constructed

"Drifting From the Design"

HAVE you ever been rudely awakened by a wall while sleepwalking? Suddenly jolted back to your senses? I have, and it's a very sickening feeling. This feeling probably best describes the shock I experienced one day during my early years of pastoring in Small Town, U.S.A.

Only a block away from our church campus, I stopped at a local convenience store, one that I visited often. I needed a cup of coffee. I *really* like coffee. Sometimes I think I even covet coffee. Maybe it could be served for communion one day. OK! OK! I'm just kidding!

As I strolled down one of the congested aisles, I met a familiar face. I nodded, said, "Hello," and then proceeded to invite her to a special event taking place at our church. After I shared with her who the speaker would be each night, I expressed how *I* felt she would be blessed by attending. In my routine state of mind I totally expected to hear a response something like, "Well, if we can get loose from our schedules..." or, "If I can get my husband to come..." But her answer was far from routine! She blurted out loud enough that someone two aisles over could have heard, "We're probably not going to come."

"Excuse me?"

She said it again, only this time more emphatically. "We're probably not going to come!"

Stunned by her response to my invitation, I lowered my voice hoping she would follow my lead and, thank the good Lord, she did. In almost a whisper I said, "Do you mind explaining to me why?"

She looked down at the floor as if studying the tile grout lines, bit her bottom lip, managed a courteous smile, and then in a very calm and methodical way, told me why.

"I came to your church one time. I arrived at what I thought was an early enough time to get a good seat. You know, not too far back, but not on the front row either. I spotted that ideal spot for my children and me about three-fourths the way down the middle aisle. So we made our way toward the pew. Without a doubt, we were a little loud getting settled in, but we did the best we could." She went on, "We had only been seated a minute when someone in the pew behind us tapped me on the shoulder and said, 'Ma'am, you can't sit here in this pew...it's for our people.'"

By now her tears were splattering on the floor right beside my own traumatized heart. I did my best to console her and assure her that we would do everything possible to ensure that what happened years ago wouldn't happen again. I explained that this kind of treatment was not the sentiments of the entire congregation. Although I spoke with as much conviction as possible, I knew she had just sketched, matted, and framed an unlimited edition of "Christian Evolution." And, still today, her emotional word-portrait hangs in the gallery of my mind, a perfect picture of the religious world.

To the best of my knowledge, she never came back, at least not during my tenure there. I've often wondered if she ever found healing for her wounds and salvation for her soul; and, if she did, could it be possible she found it in a church?

How, in the name of God, do we drift so far away from the original design? Why do we even imagine that things like "private pews" resemble the Kingdom of God? The answer? Because we have forgotten what God looks like! We have forgotten what He looks like because we have been so long away from His presence.

Home Sweet Home

One of my favorite things about traveling is arriving home. There is nothing like walking through the door and feeling the warm embrace of my beautiful wife, hearing the laughter of my children, and knowing once more I'm home and I'm blessed. I always make my way to each of the children's bedrooms to kiss them and tuck them in.

One night, while going through all the "glad you're home" rituals, my little boy reached out from under the covers and squeezed my cheeks with both of his chubby little hands. His eyes seemed to study every detail of my face. He then closed his eyes for a moment, squeezed my face tighter, and opened his eyes again. He repeated this sequence a couple of times, while I enjoyed every bit of it. I finally asked him what he was doing. He said "Daddy, while you were gone I was afraid I wouldn't remember what you looked like, so tonight I'm making sure I don't ever forget."

Israel more than once forgot what God looked like. One time, in particular, their passionate leader, in search of direction, took a trip to the mountains and left his two assistants, Aaron and Hur, in charge. Moses said, *"If any man have any matters to do, let him come unto them"* (Exod. 24:14b). After Moses went up the hill, the entire plan went downhill. While he was building a relationship with the Father on the pinnacle, his people were building a cow in the pasture.

> *When the people saw that Moses was so long in coming down from the mountain, they gathered around Aaron and said, "Come, make us gods who will go before us. As for this fellow Moses who brought us up out of Egypt, we don't know what has happened to him." Aaron answered them, "Take off the gold earrings that your wives, your sons and your daughters are wearing, and bring them to me." So all the people took off their earrings and brought them to Aaron. He took what they handed him and made it into an idol cast in the shape of a calf, fashioning it with a tool. Then they said, "These are your gods, O Israel, who brought you up out of Egypt"* (Exodus 32:1-4 NIV).

You can follow the downward spiral of Israel in three descending steps:

- Diluted leadership.

- Distorted perception.

• Deified devices (cows).

Diluted Leadership

John Maxwell, Christian author and leadership counselor, said, "Everything rises and falls on leadership." If this is true, and I believe it is, some leader in Israel goofed up. You have to point the first finger at Moses. It was not God's original plan to have to communicate through Moses, to Aaron, and then finally to the people. God wanted to speak directly to Moses and then Moses would tell the people what God said. Plain and simple! But Moses said he couldn't speak very well, so God said, "OK, if you don't want to do it, I'll get Aaron."

Now I know that *"all things work together for good..."* (Rom. 8:28), but I also know that God's original plan always works best. Under Moses' conditions Israel is now getting third generation information. The more carnal humans are between God and His audience, the more probability of error.

A simple and humorous event in my youthful years taught me the danger of dilution. Not long after my wife and I were married, we decided to build our own house. During that process I learned some extremely valuable lessons. In the framing of the house, there was a need to cut several pieces of lumber the same length. So I measured the first one and cut it. I then placed that board on top of another, marked it and cut it. Each time I would use the most recent cut board as the guide for the next cut. I did not realize, until it was too late, that each time I cut a new board, the length was getting shorter. By the time I cut the third board, it was not even close to the original measurement. So I measured and marked again, cut the board with precision, then wrote on it in bold letters

"Original—Pattern." Every measurement and mark after that was derived from the original.

It appears that Israel didn't have a clue what the original pattern looked like. This problem can be attributed to the diluted communication of their leadership.

When God spoke there was no doubt as to what He was saying. When Moses spoke, he spoke as the mouthpiece of God. By the time Aaron translated, his information lacked inspiration and his communication was absent of conviction. On top of that, Aaron's spine wasn't much stronger than well-cooked spaghetti. Now you've got favorable conditions for calf construction.

Israel had an idol in their heart and Moses had the solution in his hands—the Word and the oracles of God written in stone. God's Word is the one thing He chose to "magnify above His Name" (Ps. 138:2 paraphrased). He knew His Name required only pronunciation, but His Word required the penetration of the two-edged sword. His Name no doubt identifies the body, but His Word impacts the bones. Could this be why at Calvary the body of Christ was broken but His bones were not? The temple may have been destroyed, but the main architecture can never be. (See John 1:1-14.) We err when we can't trace our object of worship back to the written Word. In fact, as leaders, we need to understand that anything that does not tether back to the Word of God tends to construct cows.

One of my most revered mentors, T.F. Tenney, used to say that the Bible is like double-knit fabric. "If you pull a thread in Genesis, it will pucker in Revelation." Maybe we should apply this test to every ministry and program in and around the Kingdom. I'm afraid if we started pulling threads, many of them would unravel before they even came near a word from God. The truth is that many are threadbare to begin with.

A few years ago my wife and I planted a church in a small college town, and I sought advice from anywhere possible, especially successful leaders. I was privileged to have an early morning cup of coffee with Coach Eddie Robinson (the most-winning college coach in football). It was as if he discerned the answer to a question I never asked. As he looked out the window far beyond the trees and grass, he said, "Rev, every man has got to have a plan, something to refer back to, and something to hang his hat on. And when everything starts to fall apart, you just go back to your plan. That's where you hang your hat."

The Word of God should be where every leader hangs his hat. If the head of the leader is in the Word then his hat will hang there also. There is no better plan than "thus saith the Lord." We need men and women today who will exercise the imperative paradox of being strong enough to submit. Not to the voice of the multitude but to the Master. Only in this submitted state can anyone truly hear from God. It's then that His voice will resonate through a broken leader who attempts to speak mere words of a man, but when they fall on the ears of lamenting listeners they scream out—"God said"!

That's what we need: *God-said leaders, who bring about God-hungry followers, who produce God-willing results.*

Distorted Perception

It's amazing what we think God looks like. Our visual image of Him can get somewhat distorted when we've been so long removed from His presence.

"How many stars did you see last night?" the teacher asked little Daniel.

"Nine hundred and twenty-eight," he replied.

She turned to a second student and asked, "How many did you see, Marcus?"

"Only seven," he stated flatly.

Seeing the inquisitive look on Renee's face the teacher said, "Renee, why do you think Marcus saw fewer stars than Daniel?"

Renee thought for a bit and said, "I guess Marcus has a smaller window."

The images we create are all colored by the windows through which we look. The people of Israel thought a golden calf best represented God because they were still looking through an Egyptian window. When we don't daily seek God's face, we tend to fall back on the familiar.

Have you ever wondered why Jesus had to sort of "redo" the healing of the blind man? He touched him and asked, "How do you see?" The man said, "I can see, but I see men as trees walking." So Jesus touched him again. This time everything was perfect. (See Mark 8:22-25.) I asked the Lord one day, why, in all His perfection, did He have to seemingly undo a mistake? He said, "There was no mistake! The first touch healed his sight; the second touch healed his perception." There was nothing wrong with what the man saw, but there were some definite problems with the way he saw them.

It doesn't take long for a pew, a stained glass window, or even a song that was being played the night we were saved, to start looking like God. That's why we must continue to walk in the light. Today's light! There is no such thing as seeing today's revelation in yesterday's light.

We need two basic things to happen in order to prevent distorted perception. First, our eyes need to be *"anointed with eye salve*" (Rev. 3:18 paraphrased). This affects *what* we see (vision). Second, our heads need to be *"anointed with oil"* (Ps. 23:5 paraphrased). This affects the *way* we see (perspective).

Deified Devices

It was one thing for the people of Israel to build a calf to pacify their desires, but it degenerated to an even lower level when they audaciously called the calf, "[our] gods." An interesting commentary about this act follows:

> It is inconceivable that they, who but a few weeks before had witnessed such amazing demonstrations of the true God, could have suddenly sunk to such a pitch of infatuation and brutish stupidity as to imagine that human art or hands could make a god that should go before them. But it must be borne in mind, that though by election and in name they were the people of God, they were as yet, in feelings and associations, in habits and taste, little, if at all different, from Egyptians (Ezek. 20:6-10). They meant the calf to be an image—a visible sign or symbol of Yahweh, so that their sin consisted not in a breach of the FIRST but of the SECOND commandment.[1]

I've never witnessed anyone bowing in worship before a gold calf, but I have seen people leave a church because a banister or chandelier was moved, or the carpet was not their first color choice. There are some who will only attend church services if they are held on a certain day of the week or even a certain time of day, with a favorite minister in the pulpit, and only one particular church name on the sign.

My thoughts used to be that these people weren't "true worshipers," but I was wrong, extremely wrong. They worship with as much conviction and passion as anyone. The real problem is the *object* of their worship. In fact, some have a tendency to worship their worship, giving glory to the mask instead of the Master. They are more in love with the system than the Savior and more attached to the frivolous than to the Father.

When any of us deify such devices, we are only meandering where God once was and never discovering where God actually is. Constant focus on the device instead of the divine constructs a maze of mediocrity that leaves us disoriented and confused.

Sometimes, I get lost in the edifice that religion and so-called theology have built around me. I am compelled to find a place of solitude, close my eyes, and say to the Father, "Daddy, I was afraid I wouldn't remember what You looked like, so I'm making sure I don't ever forget."

Are you brave enough to stop reading right now, close this book and then your eyes, and ask the Father to give you fresh light on who He is and what He looks like; to purposefully set your affections on things above and not on things below; to purpose in your heart to no longer attempt to bend God into these devices, but to baptize these devices into God? So what, if the cows drown!

Join me and pray for the entire religious world that it would return the dignity it has stolen from divinity. Pray that many will discover the truths that you are about to uncover in these next few chapters.

Pray it sincerely!

Pray it passionately!

Please, pray it now!

Wow!

This could cause a revolution, or at least a revival!

Endnote

1. *Jamieson, Fausset, and Brown Commentary*, Electronic Database, 1997 by Biblesoft.

Epigraph

Example is not the main thing in influencing others. It is the only thing.

—*Albert Schweitzer*

Maybe the reason the grass always looks greener on the forbidden side is because we see things through the eyes of a sacred cow instead of the risen Lamb.

—*Mark Briggs*

Notes

_____

_____

_____

_____

_____

_____

_____

_____

_____

_____

_____

_____

_____

_____

_____

_____

_____

_____

_____

_____

_____

CHAPTER 3

Cows That Divide

"The Roots and Fruits of Division"

HE was a short, stocky-built man about five feet, six inches tall and had never asked for help from me, and probably not from anyone. To ask for help, he perceived, would be a definitive mark of weakness, and a man had to be strong!

As he entered my office door his shoulders were slumped forward and he was stooped over as if he needed to lower himself to fit through the opening. Obviously something had happened that made him feel even smaller than he was; and from the look on his strained and weathered face, I guessed he would have preferred to totally disappear. His once brilliant eyes were now frosted over with an empty stare implying he'd rather facilitate his absence if a viable alternative was not quickly available.

With a sweat-stained cap cradled in his trembling hands he collapsed in the chair across from my desk. Before I could get to him, in a broken and almost spasmodic voice he blurted out words I'll never forget.

"Cut-in-half," he said in a rhythm as if he was drawing his last breath between each word, "cut—in—half"!

By this time I was kneeling beside him and had my arm around him. All I could think to say was, "I'm here for you and I can help you."

He said, "You don't understand, I'm cut in half. You can only put your arms around half of me and you can only pray for half of me, because she's not here!"

Then he sank even deeper into the cushioned chair and continued to mix tears with talk about how it "used to be" and mumbling to himself about what he "could have, should have done" differently.

Over the next few days and weeks we spent much time in prayer and a little time in counsel. Priority number one was to make the "one-half" we could talk to, and the other half we could only pray for, know that there was still hope. Of course the beautiful part of this story is, in time, the two halves came together again and matured into a whole and complete God-ordained family.[1]

Divide and Conquer

It happens in families, churches, businesses, and nations. It is the signature spirit of satan. Division is guilty of producing many trees of unrighteousness. Trace the gnarled unfruitful branches of any dysfunctional organization back to the trunk of the tree, and you'll find at its very base are the seeds of disunity. The root always influences the fruit. No wonder when a marriage falls apart there are so many ripple effects—emotional unrest, job problems, and unruly children, to mention only a few. I think it's safe to say that all the atrocities of culture can be traced back to division.

If you could physically dissect this creature of division, ironically you would find it divided into two parts: *root* and *fruit*. The *root* mass is made up of: contention, convenience, and control. The poisonous *fruit* is conformity and captivity. By splitting division in half we feed it its own poison. We identify the root—which is the cause, and the fruit—which is the effect. At this point division and ultimately disunity can easily be conquered, because we can treat the cause and not just the symptom.

Root of Division

Contention or contrition—a major decision.

Correction is not only necessary but imperative. However, correction "up" is considered to be rebellion. In order for rebellion to be in control, it must overpower the present authority structure. Therefore the spirit of rebellion is always positioning itself to challenge authority. The only other element necessary for this diabolical spirit to come to total fruition is an atmosphere of dissatisfaction. When people are dissatisfied, they either rebel or repent. Of course our Father expects the latter. Rebellion produces contention while repentance exemplifies contrition. Compare the two. Look at what the Bible says about contention, *"Starting a quarrel is like breaching a dam; so drop the matter before a dispute breaks out"* (Prov. 17:14 NIV). Now look at the Lord's desire for us to display an attitude of contrition: *"The sacrifices of God are a broken spirit; a broken and contrite heart, O God, You will not despise"* (Ps. 51:17 NIV).

The nation of Israel reached this atmosphere of discontent when Rehoboam became king after his father Solomon.

So Israel has been in rebellion against the house of David to this day....Jeroboam thought to himself, "The kingdom will now likely revert to the house of David. If these people go up to offer sacrifices at the temple of the Lord in Jerusalem, they will again give their allegiance to their lord, Rehoboam king of Judah. They will kill me and return to King Rehoboam." After seeking advice, the king made two golden calves. He said to the people, "It is too much for you to go up to Jerusalem. Here are your gods, O Israel, who brought you up out of Egypt." One he set up in Bethel, and the other in Dan. And this thing became a sin; the people went even as far as Dan to worship the one there. Jeroboam built shrines on high places and appointed priests from all sorts of people, even though they were not Levites. He instituted a festival on the fifteenth day of the eighth month, like the festival held in Judah, and offered sacrifices on the altar. This he did in Bethel, sacrificing to the calves he had made. And at Bethel he also installed priests at the high places he had made. On the fifteenth day of the eighth month, a month of his own choosing, he offered sacrifices on the altar he had built at Bethel. So he instituted the festival for the Israelites and went up to the altar to make offerings (1 Kings 12:19, 26-33 NIV).

After Solomon died and his son Rehoboam had come to the throne, the murmuring started immediately. Rumblings always precede revolt. Words of discontent spread like a wind driven wild fire, fast and ferocious. The truth is, words are not even necessary to constitute a murmur. The word *murmur* implies a leak and not a complete spill. Say it and listen how it sounds. Even the phonetics sound a bit leaky. Simply put, it's a sour vocal intonation or a slight gesture with an attitude.

Murmuring usually has no problem finding a leader. Whoever will take time to listen to its seeping slander is petitioning for an opportunity to lead. Jeroboam listened; his time had come to lead.

With a new leader to crusade their cause, the northern tribes (Israel) were now ready to handle the situation with human wisdom. In their frail finite minds, this was the logical thing to do. Contentions always seem to be logical.

The rebellion of these people divided Israel into two kingdoms: the northern ten tribes retaining the name of Israel, and the southern two tribes (Judah and Benjamin), calling themselves Judah. This division lasted approximately 21 years. What should have been the age of maturity became a declining process of immaturity. Both groups eventually fell into captivity.

The creature of rebellion will search until it finds an opportunity to copulate with a simple rift of dissatisfaction, bringing about an invalid newborn of contention. Just as one adulterer finds another or one spirit of perversion finds another, so rebellion has an uncanny lust for dissatisfaction and without difficulty finds it.

*Convenience—demons of division
wear the mask of convenience.*

Hard feelings and selfish attitudes often drive people into such a state of mind that they lose all sense of reason. As soon as Rehoboam announced his intention to continue and even intensify the burden that his father had imposed, the ten northern tribes were quick and ready to respond with statements and slogans: *"Down with David and all his relatives! Let's go home! Let Rehoboam be king of his own family!"* (1 Kings 12:16 TLB). Had they stopped long enough to consider their folly, they would have realized that David was far from being their problem. Now, in spite of their deep-seated convictions concerning their greatest friend and national hero, they spoke out against him.

This sort of mental vertigo tends to make people leave those they should love and love those they should leave. This state of mind promotes convenience instead of conviction. In these times of unsteadiness, people are inclined to speak from the top of their head instead of the bottom of their heart. There is absolutely no way to hear the voice of God, when emotions racing with revenge and malice are dictating the decisions.

The litany of conveniences goes on. People take matters into their own hands when things don't go the *way* they think they should, or *when* they think they should. There is no way of "taking matters into your hands" without removing them first from the hands of God.

The first major mistake they made was taking leadership out of the hands of God. He had already promised Jeroboam a kingdom—He could have, and eventually would have, worked it out if the Israelites would have but trusted Him, had patience, and waited on His perfect plan.

When we display the fruit of patience it is indicative of our closeness to our heavenly Father. In the realm of patience, time ceases to be a factor. When "time is no more," that's the eternal realm. This eternal domain is where our Father lives. All of us can experience this realm if we take time to wait.

The second major mistake they made was attempting to change God into what *they* thought He should look like. "*After seeking advice, the king made two golden calves. He said to the people, 'It is too much* [inconvenient] *for you to go up to Jerusalem. Here are your gods...'*" (1 Kings 12:28 NIV).

We humans are quick to put God in a box. We don't like parameters applied to us, yet we try to set them around God. We fear what we don't understand so we take the part we *think* we understand, quickly frame it, and then reduce it to a size, shape, and content to which we can relate. Voilà, we have a cow, a sacred cow. Initially these new shapes we give God make it easier for us to come together for a common cause. Don't be fooled. They subtly transform from menial devices into cows that divide.

The demons of division always wear the mask of convenience. Abraham was willing to settle for an Ishmael instead of waiting on an Isaac. Isaac hastily gave the blessing to Jacob instead of Esau. When it comes time for the third generation to get its blessing, notice what happens. Jacob, according to Genesis 32, is wrestling with a *theophany*, or God-form. The theophany touched the socket of Jacob's hip and caused it to become "out of joint." Then the theophany says, "Let me go, for the day breaks." In other words, it's time for the sun to show itself and after all, isn't that what you're looking for...a little bit of daybreak? But Jacob says, "I'm not looking for daybreak, I'm looking for a relationship." He said, "I'm not going to let you go until you bless me." Unlike his fathers, he was more interested in a commitment to a long-term relationship than he was a momentary convenience.

Jacob learned a lot that day as he began his lifetime love affair with brokenness. He learned that it is more important to change than to remain stagnant. He learned that daybreak was great, but to limp in complete revelatory light is more awesome. For the limp would always stimulate his memory of the light. Many of us walk in and out of light but when we have a limp *with* the light, we are reminded of the true essence of the light. The measure of light we walk in is determined by the level of our limp.

Jesus didn't preface *"Take up your cross and follow Me"* (Mark 8:34 NKJV) with "when you find it convenient." He knew that if the crown was to sit on our head, the Cross must lie on our back.

The law was not convenient. It clearly stated that the people were to go to Jerusalem three times a year. (See Exodus 23:14; Second Chronicles 8:13.) They didn't have cars, they didn't have planes and trains, so it cost them something to be obedient to God. Jeroboam, though, made it convenient—he built them custom gods, cows at the southern border and at the northern border of the kingdom. No matter where you were in the country, going to one of these "churches" of his was closer than going all the way to Jerusalem.

Notice also that he tries to tie his religion of convenience to the historic past. *"...Here are your gods, O Israel, who brought you up out of Egypt"* (1 Kings 12:28). In fact, if you recall, when Moses was up on the mountain receiving the Ten Commandments, the people got tired of waiting for Moses to return. They told Aaron to, "build us a god for we don't know what has happened to Moses." (See Exodus 32:1-6.) Aaron built the golden calf and said to them, "These are your gods."

No doubt these people in Jeraboam's day had read about or had heard a portion of the golden calf story, but they didn't have all the truth. This is where we do a disservice to the world today when we present them partial truth and not all truth. When we study God's Word out of convenience instead of out of conviction, it's a sure-fire way to be prey for a cult.

Control—desires recognition before reconciliation.

If this people go up to do sacrifice in the house of the Lord at Jerusalem, then shall the heart of this people turn again unto their lord, even unto Rehoboam king of Judah, and they shall kill me, and go again to Rehoboam king of Judah (1 Kings 12:27).

Another perpetrator that contributes to the ugly root mass of division is called control. What Jeroboam said to this new kingdom was, "I'll make it convenient for you." What he did not say—but his actions spoke much louder than his words—was, "I want to control you." His need for control was motivated by fear, fear that if he did not create a convenient place for them to worship, they would go back to Rehoboam and pledge their allegiance to him.

Jeroboam's ulterior motive began to surface after he had successfully led Israel in revolt against Rehoboam. Up to this point, we only hear of the cause—they were being unduly oppressed. Jeroboam was just a man trying to help a poor, helpless, discouraged people who were in no way able to help themselves.

What he really wanted was a throne of his own. In fact, he took precautions to make sure that the kingdoms did not reunite. He was afraid that *"now shall the kingdom return to the house of David"* (1 Kings 12:26). He was not kingdom-minded. Control always desires recognition before reconciliation.

It's easy to find someone who has an addiction or a vice and point a finger at them and say, "How can they let that control them?" Yet all the while numerous Christians are addicted to a particular day of the week or a favorite pew. These fixtures that were originally created to merely assist us in serve the Lord are now shaming us. Many in the religious world are being controlled by what is totally out of control. These roots always wear the cloak of care to conceal the monster of control.

When true worship is tainted with devices, we become history—not living disciples of His Kingdom. The Bible says on these two commandments the rest of the law hinges, *"Love the Lord your God"* and *"Love your neighbor."* (See Mark 12:30-31 NKJV.) When we create a replacement for God, it is obvious we don't love Him. We tear down the wonderful set of connections between God and His family. Without the love of God flowing through us and into the church family, unity is not only lost but impossible to achieve.

One day while I was having lunch with John Maxwell, he said, "Mark, as your ministry grows and when people desire to get close to you, one of the most important questions you'll ask is, 'Can I trust them?'" I never forgot what John said, and have recently asked myself a similar question, "Do they want to get close so they can control me?" We have to ask that question not only about *people* but we need to ask it relative to *religious systems*—how attached to a sacred cow can we afford to become? The only thing that should control us is the power of the Holy Spirit and the divine authority as set forth in the Scriptures.

People who fall under the control of religion not only worship a cow but now wear the cow's yoke, the "unnecessary yoke."

Now therefore why tempt ye God, to put a yoke upon the neck of the disciples, which neither our fathers nor we were able to bear? But we believe that through the grace of the Lord Jesus Christ we shall be saved, even as they (Acts 15:10-11).

These people were determined to add some Jewish traditions and include them as necessities for salvation. The Bible says this was causing "no small dissension" in the church. Man has always been inclined to add burdens and yokes to what God requires; this practice continues to cause division in the Body of Christ. *"For it seemed good to the Holy Ghost, and to us, to lay upon you no greater burden than these necessary things"* (Acts 15:28).

I have always been amazed at how many denominations think it's so wrong to subtract truth from the Bible but do not hesitate a moment about adding to what the Bible says or pen the Scriptures with "personal doctrines." All of this is no more than modern Pharisaism. Many confuse bearing the yoke with carrying the Cross. The fact is, when we attempt to bear the yoke, there is no room for the Cross.

People, in attempting to take control, become totally out of control. We create unbearable burdens, while Jesus removes them. People are determined to make yokes, but Jesus is destined to take yokes away. He says, *"Come unto Me, all ye that labour and are heavy laden, and I will give you rest. Take My yoke upon you, and learn of Me; for I am meek and lowly in heart: and ye shall find rest unto your souls. For My yoke is easy, and My burden is light"* (Matt. 11:28-30).

Wow, did you get that? Following Jesus is not about control. It's about compassion and spiritual comfort, a light burden and an easy yoke. In fact, He assures us that we can trade in our man-made and self-made heavy burden and yoke for His easy yoke and light burden.

Please don't get me wrong. There are some necessary yokes that bring the right kind of control to our lives. For instance, Paul said, *"Know ye not that the unrighteous shall not inherit the kingdom of God? Be not deceived: neither fornicators, nor idolaters, nor adulterers, nor effeminate, nor abusers of themselves with mankind, nor thieves, nor covetous, nor drunkards, nor revilers, nor extortioners, shall inherit the kingdom of God"* (1 Cor. 6:9-10). Of course there are numerous other absolutes relative to the Christian walk, but these "necessary things" were meant not to bring stress but strength to the body.

When the postscripts of the letter become larger than the letter, and the postscripts outnumber the holy scripts, something is wrong. The bylaws of some denominations have evolved into an article thicker than the average size Bible. What a calamity that people could become so deceived as to think that they could legislate God into their group.

It's absolutely astonishing that even though we call the Word of God "unadulterated," "infallible," "pure," "complete," and "holy," many insist they can make it better by adding to it. If anyone is willing to make a sincere effort to search, and then be honest enough to admit his or her discovery, he or she must confess that control is the motivating factor behind all the additions and accompaniments.

Fruit of Division

Conformity—crossing over without the Cross.

He made shrines on the high places, and made priests from every class of people, who were not of the sons of Levi (1 Kings 12:31 NKJV).

Jeroboam not only made calves, but at Bethel he installed priests at the high places he had made. On the fifteenth day of the eighth month, he offered sacrifices on the altar that he had built at Bethel. The Bible says that it was a month of Jeroboam's own choosing. Of course, this festival did nothing to improve the spiritual life of the people. They were simply going through the religious motions. None of it was ordained by God. Jeroboam had elevated himself from being king and priest to being like God. He ruined his life and hundreds of thousands of others who marched with him down the road toward destruction. He wanted to protect his kingdom, and the people wanted something convenient. They all got what they wanted.

However, the very security that Jeroboam sought was lost because of his refusal to trust the Almighty. His epitaph in First Kings chapter 13 reads that Jeroboam did not change his evil ways but once more appointed priests for the high places from all sorts of people. If anyone had so much as a desire to become a priest, he consecrated them. This sin of the house of Jeroboam led to its downfall and to its destruction from the face of the earth.

It's a natural step to go from rebellion to idolatry. When people rebel, they deny God His rightful place and replace

Him, usually with their own personal or custom gods. By undermining authority they take the place of final authority. No wonder Samuel told Saul that his *"rebellion was as witch-craft and his iniquity as idolatry."* (See First Samuel 15:23 NKJV.) In those days, idols were made of material things such as wood and stone. In our day, idols can range from careers to appearance, but the foundation of rebellion is the same— rejecting God's authority. The same principle is found in witchcraft and idolatry.

The devil wants to do all he can to keep people from truly worshiping Jesus; because when true worship exists, people stay focused on who the true God is. Satan knows that if people really pray and worship as they should, and seek the truth within the Word of God, they will no longer be rebellious. So he causes people to focus on a division rather than on the Deliverer. When people think of worshiping as enthusiastical-ly as they did when they first believed, the devil reminds them of trouble they've been through. Even if all the pieces were put back together, he lures them with pride to hold them back from obedience to God's Word.

When people are thinking spiritually they recognize satan's schemes. When they are constantly looking at a God of right-eousness and purity, they can discern unrighteousness and impurity and do not submit to an evil leader's tactics. But notice how perversion progresses. After the people are in a state of rebellion, the unqualified leader has a freedom he could not have exercised beforehand.

After the followers of Jeroboam turned away from God's directions, Jeroboam *"made priests from every class of people, who were not of the sons of Levi."* The people of God would never have accepted this blatant disregard for God's laws a few short years before. But now they have not only distorted vision, but they also have blind minds. It's startling what we will settle for when we've been detached from the real God. The Bible says that Jeroboam *"devised in his own heart"* a sacrifice and a time of sacrifice, according to First Kings 12:33.

Herein lies the problem; we cannot trust our own hearts unless it is directed toward the Father. Once the heart's direction is turned away from the Father, then we are open to conformity and once conformity sets in, there is no limit as to how far it can take us. That's why the apostle Paul directed us to *"not be conformed to this world but* [to] *be transformed by the renewing of* [the] *mind"* (Rom. 12:2 NKJV). The only thing a non-renewed mind can do is conform. On the other hand, through worship, which we will talk about later, we renew our minds and are transformed into His likeness. Where honest, true worship is prevalent, there can be no conformity.

It is true we can redefine our methods without demolishing our message. However, in the process of crossing over, let's make sure that we bring the Cross over. Crossing over without the Cross only means compromise. The question is, what is compromise? Christian author and scholar John Fischer writes:

> Worldly compromise is so hard to define. It's not an issue that you easily identify, fight, picket, or bomb...it's slippery, it's elusive; it conceals itself in the highest places and wraps its evil tentacles around the most bedrock truth. It disguises itself with much good intention and when uncovered, it excuses itself repeatedly with helpless cries of fatalism. Compromise is primarily a heart issue and this is what makes it so hard to find. How do you examine the heart?[2]

A heart issue is exactly what it was for Jeroboam. Because of the contention, the convenience, and his desire to control, the fruit of conformity ripened throughout the land. Initially it was palatable, but how quickly it became a soured rotten apple. Thomas J. Watson of IBM said,

> Strangely, the expounders of many of the great new ideas of history were frequently considered on the lunatic fringe for some or all of their lives. If one stands up and is counted from time to time, one may get knocked down. But remember, a man flattened by an opponent can get up again, a man flattened by conformity stays down for good.[3]

Captivity—when God hides.

Approximately 21 years after Jeroboam took the throne, both kingdoms—Judah and Israel—were taken captive, one by the Assyrians, the other by the Babylonians. Both the root and the fruit of division cunningly united in order to divide.

Disunity always leads to captivity. Under the banner of liberty and freedom, we build walls that divide, then we are made captive by our own creations. Within the box where we keep God, these new shapes we give Him initially unite us. But, like Jeroboam's cows, these improper points of focus quickly transform into insulting points of failure. When division is inevitable, divinity becomes invisible. What a tragedy when God hides.

If we want to avoid captivity, we must avoid disunity. The best way to fight disunity is with unity. Psalm 133 gives us the grand recipe for unity.

Behold, how good and how pleasant it is for brethren to dwell together in unity! It is like the precious ointment upon the head, that ran down upon the beard, even Aaron's beard: that went down to the skirts of his garments; as the dew of Hermon, and as the dew that descended upon the mountains of Zion: for there the Lord commanded the blessing, even life for evermore (Psalm 133:1-3).

It's all about the oil, the crushing and the breaking. When we're crushed and broken we bring a sweet smelling aroma. Individually we are stench in the nostrils of God; but, crushed and broken, in the collective parts, we come into a oneness with Him and He cannot hide. Not until we are willing to be divided individually can we be united collectively. Unity attracts God like nothing else, because nothing reflects His character better.

I very seldom read the newspaper, much less the cartoons; but if I read the cartoons I want to keep up with "Peanuts." In one particular "Peanuts" cartoon, Lucy demands that Linus change the TV channel. Then she threatens him with her fist in the air if he doesn't do so swiftly.

"What makes you think you can walk right in here and take over?" asks Linus.

"These five fingers," says Lucy. "Individually they're nothing but when I curl them like this into a single unit, they form a weapon that is terrible to behold."

"Which channel do you want?" asks Linus. Turning away he looks at his fingers and says, "Why can't you guys get organized like that?"

Jesus prayed, *"that all of them may be one, Father, just as You are in Me and I am in You. May they also be in Us so that the world may believe that You have sent Me*" (John 17:21 NIV). Christ was not praying for a *work of* unity but a *walk in* unity. When we come together for an event, cause, or program, this is a *work of* unity. When we come together in Him, this is a *walk in* unity. The first is institutional, the second is relational. Men like Hitler and Stalin demanded and experienced institutional unity—extreme examples; but unfortunately, institutional unity is the only unity many Christians will ever experience. This type of unity is, however, not what Jesus was praying for when He prayed *"that all of them may be one."* He was praying for relational unity. In this ultimate state of unity, Christ is the focus and not the program, which eliminates bouts of personal puffiness.

At low tide there are multitudes of separated pools along the shore. But at high tide they flow together and the little distinctions are lost in one splendid union. What we need to pray for is high tide so all the distinctive parts of the Body of Christ can flow together in one wonderful, glorious ocean. Now wouldn't that be a dream come true? If this were to happen, just imagine how many other ideas would be activated.

Recently a group of orchestra violinists were suing for a pay raise, claiming they play many more notes per concert than do their colleagues. The 16 violinists point to their less busy colleagues who play flute, oboe, or trombone.[4]

In many ways the modern church is like a segregated orchestra. The last thing we need is prima donnas or people who keep track of notes. If we don't learn to resonate with harmony, we are sure to obliterate with hatred.

I would ask one favor of you before you read any farther. Please stop and analyze your life right now. See if there is a sacred cow nestled somewhere in your belief system, a sacred cow that could cause division among your brothers and sisters in the Lord. Look for a cow that initially seemed insignificant, but now demands to be served and looms over you daily, dictating your every step and decision. It even taints your hunger for more of God, because you are so busy feeding the cow instead of discovering the King.

What a tragedy to find yourself at the end of your life and suddenly realize that petty and unimportant things prevented you from having wonderful and glorious fellowship with other believers—and your heavenly Father. Stop and take notice of how many times our Lord drew the circle as large as possible to be inclusive. Even during times when the Pharisees wanted Him to make the loop strict and small, He refused. He modeled inclusion, not exclusion. Exclusion divides and division ultimately brings about captivity. Inclusion unifies and provides opportunity for genuine liberty.

When the called-out ones—the Church—come into perfect unity, producing that sweet aroma, we can say, as Christ said, *"When you've seen Me, you've seen My Father"* (see John 14:9). Then and only then will we know perfect unity.

"We have never achieved perfect unity in a local church any more than any of us has been completely transformed into the image of Christ." [5] Knowing how to identify the roots and fruits of division is the first step toward unity. Eliminating the cows in our lives and ripping off the masks that keep us hidden from our heavenly Father are the first steps toward transforming into the image of Christ.

Endnotes

1. This is a composite story, a compilation of several pastoral experiences. This composite protects the privacy of those involved.

2. "Contemporary Christian Music", February 1987, *Christianity Today*, Volume 31, No. 11.

3. Thomas J. Watson, Jr., "From the Chairman of the Board of IBM Corporation," *Leadership*, Volume 1, No. 1.

4. "Violinists Say Pay Far from Noteworthy," *Chicago Tribune*, 24 March 2004.

5. Truman Dollar, *Leadership*, Volume 7, No. 4.

Epigraph

A man is a method, a progressive arrangement; a selecting principle gathering his like unto him wherever he goes. What you are comes to you.

—*Ralph Waldo Emerson*

Sometimes I think Jesus' words "wars and rumors of wars" are more applicable to the wars in and about religion than anything else.

—*Mark Briggs*

Notes

_____

_____

_____

_____

_____

_____

_____

_____

_____

_____

_____

CHAPTER 4

Cows That Grow

"Party Animals"

EVEN when she was a toddler, my oldest daughter had a fascination with cameras and photography. So my wife and I bought her a camera for her birthday. We thought it would soothe her itch, so to speak, but instead, she broke out in hives! Before the birthday party was over she took so many pictures that the entire roll of film was used. We finally had to limit how many pictures she could take, because we couldn't support her habit.

Then we advanced to digital. What a wonderful breakthrough! She could snap as many pictures as her little fingers could handle. And did she ever take advantage of that freedom!

The digital camera gift idea was wonderful, until recently. This intelligent daughter, now nearly 20, complained about her computer responding slowly. So, I checked it out. You can guess what I found: file on top of file of photographs, downloaded from the digital camera to the hard drive of her

computer, slowing the response time incredibly. I even discovered some photos that she slipped in on my laptop. The
good news is she has her growing-up life in pictures, from
about seven years old until now. And that's a great album of
memories!

The Gallery

Jesus taught with pictures, word pictures known as para-
bles that allowed anyone who desired to see into the very heart
and character of God. Looking in and through the frame of
Christ we can see some of the minute details of God. After all,
He is the "express image of the portrait of God, and is stamped
with the nature of God and holds the picture together with His
words." (See Hebrews 1:3.)

I am a fourth-generation student of the Bible, and for years
I have gazed into the gallery of many New Testament exhibits.
But no portraits are painted any clearer than the ones produced by Christ in the Gospel of Luke, chapter 15. An ideal
name for this animated showcase would be "The Lost and
Found Gallery." Think about it. each character, with the excep-
tion of the Father, experienced a feeling of being lost.

Walk with Luke and me and let's observe these breathtak-
ing sketches together. I have given each one a unique and
applicable name so they can be easily recognized in the present and remembered in the future. Deliberately, I've wasted
no stroke of the word brush, so please r-e-a-d s-l-o-w-l-y.
Savor each word, chew it until you taste it, and hold it until
you feel it,

For the purpose of descriptive interpretation, please allow
me to interject the characters' names into the scriptural set-

ting. As you view their imprint, you can also realize their implications.

> *Now the tax collectors and* [Leonard Sinner and his friends] *were all gathering around to hear Him. But the* [Fair-u-see Family] *and the teachers of the law muttered, "This man welcomes sinners and eats with them."*
>
> *Then Jesus told them this parable: "Suppose one of you has a hundred sheep and loses one of them* [Wandering Wool]. *Does he not leave the ninety-nine in the open country and go after* [Wandering Wool] *until he finds it? And when he finds it, he joyfully puts it on his shoulders and goes home. Then he calls his friends and neighbors together and says, 'Rejoice with me; I have found my lost sheep.' I tell you that in the same way there will be more rejoicing in heaven over one sinner who repents than over ninety-nine righteous persons who do not need to repent.*
>
> *"Or suppose a woman has ten silver coins and loses one. Does she not light a lamp, sweep the house and search carefully until she finds* [Sincere Silver]*? And when she finds it, she calls her friends and neighbors together and says, 'Rejoice with me; I have found my lost coin.' In the same way, I tell you, there is rejoicing in the presence of the angels of God over one sinner who repents."*
>
> *Jesus continued: "There was a man who had two sons.* [Yancy Younger] *said to his father, 'Father, give me my share of the estate.' So he divided his property between them.*

"Not long after that, [Yancy] got together all he had, set off for a distant country and there squandered his wealth in wild living. After he had spent everything, there was a severe famine in that whole country, and he began to be in need. So he went and hired himself out to a citizen of that country, who sent him to his fields to feed pigs. He longed to fill his stomach with the pods that the pigs were eating, but no one gave him anything.

"When he came to his senses, he said, 'How many of my father's hired men have food to spare, and here I am starving to death! I will set out and go back to my father and say to him: Father, I have sinned against heaven and against you. I am no longer worthy to be called your son; make me like one of your hired men.' So he got up and went to his father.

"But while he was still a long way off, his father saw him and was filled with compassion for him; he ran to [Yancy], threw his arms around him and kissed him.

"[Yancy] said to him, 'Father, I have sinned against heaven and against you. I am no longer worthy to be called your son.'

"But the father said to his servants, 'Quick! Bring the best robe and put it on him. Put a ring on his finger and sandals on his feet. Bring the [Fat Calf] and kill it. Let's have a feast and celebrate. For this son of mine was dead and is alive again; he was lost and is found.' So they began to celebrate.

"Meanwhile, [Ollie Older] was in the field. When he came near the house, he heard music and dancing. So he called one of the servants and asked him what

*was going on. 'Your brother has come,' he replied,
'and your father has killed the* [Fat Calf] *because he
has him back safe and sound.'*

"[Ollie Older] *became angry and refused to go in. So
his father went out and pleaded with him. But he
answered his father, 'Look! All these years I've been
slaving for you and never disobeyed your orders. Yet
you never gave me even a young goat so I could celebrate with my friends. But when this son of yours
who has squandered your property with prostitutes
comes home, you kill the* [Fat Calf] *for him!'*

" '[Ollie Older],' *the father said, 'you are always with
me, and everything I have is yours. But we had to
celebrate and be glad, because this brother of yours*
[Yancy Younger] *was dead and is alive again; he was
lost and is found' "* (Luke 15:1-32 NIV).

Gallery Observations

Leonard Sinner—Often singled out and criticized. Most
people overlook his value, which to be appreciated must be
seen in the Light. Although one of a kind, new ones are being
drawn every day—each having its own unique characteristics
and incredible value.

*Now the tax collectors and "sinners" were all gather-
ing around to hear Him. But the Pharisees and the
teachers of the law muttered, "This man welcomes
sinners and eats with them."*

Fair-u-see Family—A beautiful picture of the alphabet with perfectly dotted i's and painstakingly crossed t's. But look closer—there's one major flaw. A new alphabet has been introduced: the Alpha and Omega, and they don't recognize it (Him).

Now the tax collectors and sinners were all gathering around to hear Him. But the "Pharisees" and the teachers of the law muttered, "This man welcomes sinners and eats with them."

Wandering Wool—A great one for those who suffer with insomnia. After looking deep into this one, you will never have trouble when counting sheep. There is only one—you should feel privileged.

Suppose one of you has a hundred sheep and loses one of them. Does he not leave the ninety-nine in the open country and go after the lost sheep until he finds it?

Sincere Silver—Only when it's isolated and viewed in candlelight can you read the tarnished inscription: "It's not my fault." There are at least nine other pieces that look almost identical but are not nearly as valuable, because no one knows their story.

Or suppose a woman has ten silver coins and loses one. Does she not light a lamp, sweep the house and search carefully until she finds it?

Yancy Younger—A portrait of youth, painted in oil, allowing slower drying time for more workability. He has been most recently framed with choices. (Good ones.) The original framed portrait, also made from choices, was donated to a hog farmer.

Not long after that, the younger son got together all he had, set off for a distant country and there squandered his wealth in wild living. After he had spent everything, there was a severe famine in that whole country, and he began to be in need. So he went and hired himself out to a citizen of that country, who sent him to his fields to feed pigs. He longed to fill his stomach with the pods that the pigs were eating, but no one gave him anything.

Ollie Older—Per his request, he wanted his portrait to show the old home in the background. But as you can see, though he stands near the front door, the Father's house still appears to be many miles away.

Meanwhile, the older son was in the field. When he came near the house, he heard music and dancing. So he called one of the servants and asked him what was going on.

Fat Calf—This one is always dying to help.

"Bring the fattened calf and kill it. Let's have a feast and celebrate."

Father—The only backdrop is all of the other artwork. This one alone is the focal point of the entire collage. This is the Shepherd who left the 99 for only one. This is the Sweeper of the house to find one coin. And this is the "Certain Man" who suffered two boys leaving home, one geographically, the other emotionally and spiritually. This is the Father who patiently waited for both to return and is ready and willing to throw a party no matter what the cost.

> *But the father said to his servants, "Quick! Bring the best robe and put it on him. Put a ring on his finger and sandals on his feet. Bring the fattened calf and kill it. Let's have a feast and celebrate. For this son of mine was dead and is alive again; he was lost and is found." So they began to celebrate.*

As I ponder this powerful lesson-loaded story, I resist the temptation to disclose the many more numerous things it speaks to us and simply point out that Jesus had one colossal purpose in mind. He intended to show the Father's concern and compassion for unworthy sinners, but also to condemn the attitude of the arrogant and conceited religionists, the self-appointed gauges of godliness. The prodigal's elder brother represents the Scribes and Pharisees. In fact, "*Their grumbling triggered this story*" (Luke 15:3 TM).

The Pharisees felt it was their responsibility to expurgate the life of Christ. These self-appointed cleansers were the insurers of all that's fair-u-see. They interpreted "*whosoever will, let him come*" to mean "whosoever will, let him check with us first."

The elder brother's spirit was not just similar to the Pharisee spirit; it was the spirit. The elder didn't have a problem with the ring, the robe or the shoes—just don't kill that calf! His own words were, "You never killed the calf for me!"

Causes for the "Don't Kill the Cow" Attitude

No relationship with the Father

Meanwhile, the older son was in the fields working; when he returned home, he heard dance music coming from the house, and he asked one of the servants what was going on (Luke 15:25-26 TLB).

Asking the yard-workers what's going on in our own house indicates a weak or non-existent relationship with the Father. If this older brother had any kind of connection, he would have known, as soon as he heard the music, that the party was about his brother's coming home. It's very hard to think like the Father when we haven't seen the Father. John said, "*When Christ is openly revealed, we'll see him—and in seeing him, become like him*" (1 John 3:2b TM).

Some dear friends of my wife and mine adopted a little girl, and it has been very interesting watching her grow up. She is not biologically related to either parent, but after years of being disciplined and loved by them, she has many of her mother and father's characteristics. Likewise, our resemblance to the Father is dependant on how often we hang out with Him.

Whether I'm ministering at my home church where I pastor, or as a guest in another city, I teach and preach that every person should have a church to call home and a place in which to worship on a regular basis. There is no substitute for this. But I also teach that this does not take the place of private time with the Father. If we're not careful, we start taking on the appearance of the denomination that facilitates us instead of the divinity that shapes us. Attending church gives us a structure, but spending time with the Father gives us a Savior.

When I see my heavenly Father in the light of the prodigal story, I see better than ever His desire to give "good and perfect gifts." In fact, predicated on this story, we can see His gifting in three dimensions of relationship:

- The compassion dimension

- The companion dimension

- The celebration dimension

The Compassion Dimension

Throughout the Bible it is either spoken or implied that Christ was moved with compassion prior to any miraculous happening. This is the spirit of the Father. No wonder Jesus could say, "*I and the Father are one*" (John 10:30 NIV).

This level of relationship is entry level. It is where He gives us hugs and kisses and congratulates us for deciding to come back. This is what I call the "Honey, I'm home" level. Basic gifts of compassion, but nothing intimate, are distributed. If you're saved, you can relate to this dimension.

There is something you should know about this level.

This is the dimension where the Father *runs*.

But while he was still a long way off, his father saw him and was filled with compassion for him; he ran to his son, threw his arms around him and kissed him.

If He runs in the compassion dimension, can you imagine what He does in the more intimate levels?

The Companion Dimension

We are introduced to this level when we enter where the Father lives. This is where He shares with us all of the numerous heirlooms. It's here where we learn the privileges of sonship.

But the father said to his servants, "Quick! Bring the best robe and put it on him. Put a ring on his finger and sandals on his feet."

With the ring, He empowers us—authority.

With the robe, He includes us—fellowship.

With the shoes, He releases us—evangelism.

This is the dimension where the Father shares.

The Celebration Dimension

What appears to be a small, insignificant fuzzy-headed animal out behind the barn is actually an important tool and symbol of celebration in the Kingdom. The calf's destiny of death is to bring life to the party. If it doesn't die, the party doesn't live.

"Bring the fattened calf and kill it. Let's have a feast and celebrate. For this son of mine was dead and is alive again; he was lost and is found." So they began to celebrate.

With the calf, He celebrates with us—worship.

This is the ultimate relationship with the Father. This is what He lives for.

This is the dimension where the Father dances. We will discuss this level in much more detail in a later chapter dealing with worship.

When we make our way back home, holding our broken and contrite heart in our slop-stained hands, all of Heaven stops to celebrate. There is only one thing left for us to do—accept the gifts and enjoy the party.

The older brother had no concept of this kind of relationship; therefore, he resented the party for the brother. Although he was working for the father, at some point he stopped walking with the father—producing a "don't kill the cow" attitude.

No fellowship with the brother

The next time you go to your favorite sporting event, observe the referee. Do you think he has a favorite team? Who can tell? Does it look like he's having a good time? Not hardly! In fact he appears to have a chip on his shoulder. An entire bag of chips! And they're not for the party afterward, because he can't celebrate. You'll never see him giving a high five to the other refs. No! Just follow the rules and no celebration. The referee has two main purposes: keep the rules and keep the score.

This is the spirit of the older brother, which is not akin to the father's. Consequently this rules-and-score attitude prevents fellowship with the brother.

As far as we know, the first question God asked man was "Where are you?" And the second question was, "Where is your brother?" Therefore, the two most important things in our life should be developing relationship with our Father and pursuing fellowship with our brother.

After more than 20 years of being a pastor, I have noticed that, if there is a chronic fellowship problem with Bill and George, and another problem with Bill and John, and yet another with Bill and Sam, there is most definitely a relationship problem with Bill and God.

If a man say, I love God, and hateth his brother, he is a liar: for he that loveth not his brother whom he hath seen, how can he love God whom he hath not seen? (1 John 4:20)

If I am my Father's son, then I must be my brother's keeper. Calvary epitomized an incredible intersection of relationship and fellowship. At this crossroad of vertical and horizontal is where all brothers must live.

No discipleship as a son

When there is no discipline, there can be no joy. If the older brother had been about the Father's business, he would have been prepared for the homecoming. He was not only ill prepared, he was ill with resentment. He detested the celebration because rules had been broken and somebody should have to pay! (That's only Fair-u-see...that same Pharisee spirit.)

What he failed to realize is that keeping the rules doesn't necessarily constitute discipleship. In fact, true discipleship needs no rules, but passionately pursues the favor of the Father—working so close to Him that when He breathes you understand exactly what He is saying, and when He doesn't, you can only tremble.

When you work near the Father and are disciplined to do His will, you can be part of the glorious celebration and enjoy all its amenities with your brother. *"He that goeth forth and weepeth, bearing precious seed, shall doubtless come again rejoicing, bringing his sheaves with him"* (Ps. 126:6).

Stop the Sourdough

Christ used the word leaven to describe the Pharisees. He tells His disciples, in Luke 12:1, to *"beware...of the leaven of the Pharisees...."* Of course, He knew there was a Judas among them and realized that this swelling sourdough spirit could not be allowed to "leaven the whole lump."

If you'll notice, the Lord addresses the disciples first. *"Be on your guard,"* He says, *"against the* [leaven] *of the Pharisees, which is hypocrisy"* (Luke 12:1b NIV).[1] The disciples represent the family of God. They were the cream of the crop, and yet He says to them, "Be careful that it doesn't get into the family."

There are two things that without fail cause a sourdough spirit to rise in a local congregation—compassion and celebration. Anytime compassion is exercised, celebration is inevitable. On the other hand, if compassion is limited, "leaven" is probable.

If I were to compile a list of all the antichrist spirits that I've encountered in my years of ministry, a judgmental spirit would top the list. I strongly feel it is the first sign of lukewarmness. Unfortunately, this spirit manifests itself when a body of believers reaches out with a compassionate (missions) spirit or when the celebration (worship) goes to a new level.

One of the disciplines that is imperative for Christians to learn is the restraint of judgment. It's easy to stand on this side of Luke 15 and say, "Oh, I would never." But the truth is, if we don't keep our carnal nature crucified, a judgmental spirit is inevitable.

Any time you exclaim judgment you exclude joy! A judgmental spirit incarcerates celebration.

Remember the woman who broke the alabaster box? There were people watching who had the "don't kill the cow" spirit, but Jesus said, "Leave her alone; against the day of my burial has she done this" (John 12:7, my paraphrase). She obviously had a greater vision of what was coming than some of Christ's closest followers. People who lavish on Him extravagantly simply have a greater revelation of Him.

Fat Calves Must Die or...

The fattened calf was to be consumed. I've heard it said that the calf had been there waiting and ready for the prodigal to come home ever since the day he left. In truth, several calves may have come and gone. Because calves have a way of quickly becoming cows. To be true producers in God's Kingdom, we must allow Him to be a consumer of our own.

And they that are Christ's have crucified the flesh with the affections and lusts. If we live in the Spirit, let us also walk in the Spirit. Let us not be desirous of vain glory, provoking one another, envying one another (Galatians 5:24-26).

"All of heaven rejoices over one sinner coming to repentance" (Luke 15:7, my paraphrase.) When we are born into the Kingdom of God, each of us is given a "calf" to consume, and when we consume (put it to use: gifts, talents, etc.), then we get another and another and so on. We stop getting "calves" (blessing, joy, fulfillment) when we allow these calves to become cows. Fat calves must die, or sacred cows will live.

Remember: good cows die young! When our calf (system) is slain, only then can the Father celebrate.

Is Your Father Dancing Yet?

One of the most interesting stories in the Bible is that of the delivering of the talents. Five talents were given to one man, two talents to another, and a single talent to a third. The two individuals who saw growth from the talents were the ones who were willing to put them to use. Notice the attitude of the one-talent man in Matthew 25:24, *"Then he which had received the one talent came and said, Lord, I knew thee that thou art an hard man, reaping where thou hast not sown, and gathering where thou hast not strawed."*

He was concentrating so much on the rule keeping that he forgot about redemption. Merely preserving things that God has given us is not enough. Programs and systems that have been delivered to the church for a season must not become sacred. This man was so focused on preservation that he missed the whole point. He was called an "unprofitable" servant and destroyed. The bottom line: either we destroy our cows, or we will be obliterated.

You can hang out with the cows if you so desire. I've discovered that the Father lives not in the barnyard, but in the Father's house. No doubt you'll find His tracks out by the calf lot near the barn, but you will not find Him there. He gathers what He needs for service and goes back to the house, hoping to find you there. You'll find only service items at the barn. But you will find Savior things in the "Father's house."

Listen, I think I hear music and dancing. Let's go home and celebrate! All I ask is one favor. As you walk up the front porch steps, venture a peek at the lot by the barn. Do you see what I see?

A new calf!

I hope he's nervous.

Endnote

1. See Luke 12:1-12, *Matthew Henry's Commentary on the Whole Bible*: New Modern Edition, Electronic Database. Copyright (c) 1991 by Hendrickson Publishers, Inc.:

   II. The instructions, which he gave his followers, in the hearing of this auditory.

   1. He began with a caution against hypocrisy. This he said to his disciples first of all, either to the twelve, or to the seventy. These were his more peculiar charge, his family, his school, and therefore he particularly warned them as his beloved sons; they made more

profession of religion than others and hypocrisy in that was the sin they were most in danger of. They were to preach to others; and, if they should prevaricate, corrupt the word, and deal deceitfully, hypocrisy would be worse in them than in others. Besides, there was a Judas among them, who was a hypocrite, and Christ knew it, and would hereby startle him, or leave him inexcusable. Christ's disciples were, for aught we know, the best men then in the world, yet they needed to be cautioned against hypocrisy. Christ said this to the disciples, in the hearing of this great multitude, rather than privately when he had them by themselves, to add the greater weight to the caution, and to let the world know that he would not countenance hypocrisy, no, not in his own disciples. Now observe,

(1.) The description of that sin which he warns them against: It is the leaven of the Pharisees.

[1.] It is leaven; it is spreading as leaven, insinuates itself into the whole man, and all that he does; it is swelling and souring as leaven, for it puffs men up with pride, embitters them with malice, and makes their service unacceptable to God.

[2.] It is the leaven of the Pharisees: "It is the sin they are most of them found in. Take heed of imitating them; be not you of their spirit; do not dissemble in Christianity as they do in Judaism; make not your religion a cloak of maliciousness, as they do theirs."

Epigraph

Forgiveness—the most selfish thing anyone could ever do. (Think about that.)

—*Mark Briggs*

Too many Christians are no longer fishers of men but keepers of the aquarium.

—*Paul Harvey*

To maintain a herd of sacred cows, you must develop a warm and affectionate relationship with fence posts and barbed wire.

—*Mark Briggs*

Notes

_____

_____

_____

_____

_____

_____

_____

_____

_____

_____

_____

CHAPTER 5

Cows That Kill

"Chariot Chasing and Shadow Casting"

BARBARA Newbury[1] clicked off the television, and slammed the remote down on the coffee table in front of her.

"That's it!" she exclaimed. "We're not eating any more beef in this house!"

She and her husband, Gerald, had just been watching a BBC news report about an outbreak of "mad cow disease," more correctly known as bovine spongiform encephalopathy (BSE), and its human counterpart, a rare brain disorder called Creutzfeldt-Jakob Disease (CJD).

The video of the incinerating of mountains of potentially infected cattle had been disturbing, but even more haunting had been the personal interviews of the family members of victims of this tragically fatal disease.

"Aw, Babs, simmer down," Gerald said angrily. "You're always over-reacting! We are not going to change our entire lifestyle just because you've got a bee in your bonnet over some stupid news story!"

"Why, Gerry, where did that outburst come from? You never talk to me like that!"

"Aw, can it!" he snarled as he stomped out of the room.

Barbara sat in stunned silence. Gerald's irritability had become a growing problem in their relationship in recent weeks. Where had her mild-mannered husband gone, and who was this ill-tempered grouch who had taken his place?

Gerald's outburst had almost overshadowed her concern over the news story, but as she rehearsed the scenes in her mind, a foreboding gloom settled over her. Little did she know it was a premonition of the horrors that would fill the coming weeks.

A couple of days later, Gerald called Barbara from the doctor's office to ask her to pick him up and bring him home.

"What's wrong, Gerry?"

"Aw, nothing much. I was playing racquetball, and twisted my ankle. My feet have been hurting a lot lately, and I guess I just overdid it. The doctor also gave me some pills to help me sleep."

Barbara had noticed that Gerald had not been sleeping well recently, often tossing and moaning throughout the night. She had attributed his irritability to lack of sleep.

Well, she thought to herself, *maybe this is for the best. Maybe his attitude will improve.*

But the sleeping pills did not seem to help, and Gerald's feet became increasingly painful. His regular schedule of playing racquetball three times a week became a random game every other week or so, and these outings were always followed by considerable complaining of pain and fatigue. Barbara became increasingly concerned as she watched her normally healthy and lively mate become more and more inactive.

A few weeks later, Barbara noticed that Gerald's speech had become slurred, his handwriting was shaky, and he was unsteady on his feet. She insisted that he visit the doctor again, and finally he relented. By this time, his ill temper had subsided somewhat; in fact, he had become withdrawn and moody.

The doctor x-rayed Gerald's feet, but found no abnormalities. He referred Gerald to the rheumatology clinic at the hospital, but tests there showed nothing wrong either. Gerald was then sent to a neurologist, but again, all the specialists' efforts were fruitless.

Over the next month, Gerald's condition rapidly deteriorated. He ate very little and his weight dropped dramatically. He could not remember names and other important bits of information. He experienced severe panic attacks that caused him to gasp for air. Barbara feared he was developing asthma.

And then the hallucinations started. Sometimes Gerald would tell stories that were pure fantasy. Other times, it was obvious that he was trying to make connections between unrelated bits of information. Barbara grieved as she listened to these incoherent babblings.

Her concern turned to desperation as she watched her husband deteriorate right in front of her eyes. She could get no answers from the medical community, and her practical, commonsense approach to life was this time producing no solutions to the dilemma. In the midst of the ever increasing crises of the moment, she had totally forgotten the haunting news story about the "mad cows."

After a stay in the hospital Gerald's condition worsened— he could no longer walk and had become incontinent.

Barbara became overwhelmed with the responsibility of caring for him, and he was once again admitted to the hospital. This time the psychotherapist, who had previously diagnosed Gerald as suffering from deep depression and hyper-anxiety disorder, now told Barbara that he feared Gerald had a progressive degenerative neurological disease. Nothing could be done to save him—Gerald's death was inevitable.

Barbara naturally rejected this diagnosis and immediately sought a second opinion. But the new diagnosis was worse than the first, not because it was any different, but because it was so specific. Gerald had CJD and there was no hope of recovery.

Fortunately, Gerald did not suffer long. He was transferred to a hospice facility and succumbed to the disease. But his death was not the end of problems for the Newbury family. Barbara, who had never resorted to medications to help her through life's trials, now found herself able to cope only with the aid of sleeping pills and depression medication. Hers was now a life filled with counselors and psychiatrists, and as the dosages increased, her spirit sank lower as she tried to make sense of her husband's death.

Mad Cow Disease

"Mad cow disease," or BSE, is a fatal brain disorder that occurs in cattle and is caused by some unknown agent. In BSE, the unknown agent causes the cow's brain cells to die, forming sponge-like holes in the brain. The cow behaves strangely and eventually dies. The connection between BSE and humans was uncovered in Great Britain in the 1990s when several young people died of CJD, a rare human brain disorder that typically strikes only elderly people. The new variation, nvCJD, was found to be similar to BSE based on the following findings:[2]

- The nvCJD victims had lived in areas where outbreaks of BSE had occurred in cattle years earlier. No victims were found in areas without BSE outbreaks.

- The brains of nvCJD victims had proteins called *prions* (pronounced "pree-ahnz") that were similar to those from the brains of BSE-infected cows, but different from those found in victims of classic CJD.

- The time between the BSE outbreaks and the deaths of the victims was similar to the time that it takes for CJD to develop.

The British government concluded that BSE was probably the cause of nvCJD, and that the victims probably contracted the disease by eating meat from BSE-infected cows.

Both BSE and nvCJD are characterized by a long incubation period of up to several years, during which there is no visible indication of the disease. The incubation period for BSE among cattle ranges from three to eight years; for nvCJD among humans, the incubation period is unknown, but is at least five years and could extend up to 20 years or longer. The diseases are invariably fatal; there is no known treatment or cure.

The source of the BSE problem in Great Britain is still uncertain, but the outbreak in 1996 was almost certainly brought on by the practice of feeding cattle with meat-and-bone meal *made from cows.*

To contain the disease, the British government took a number of steps, including the institution of a feed ban prohibiting the use of meat-and-bone meal and slaughtering all cattle believed to be infected.

A few observations about this phenomenon merit our attention.

A Form of Cannibalism

First, "mad cow disease" was the result of feeding cow herds with an unnatural diet. Cows are herbivores, yet these cows were being fed a protein-enriched diet made from reprocessing the meat and bones of their own kind—a form of *cannibalism*!

We cannot help but remember the admonition of Paul to the Galatians concerning relationships among Christians.

> *For, brethren, ye have been called unto liberty; only use not liberty for an occasion to the flesh, but by love serve one another. For all the law is fulfilled in one word, even in this; Thou shalt love thy neighbour as thyself.* **But if ye bite and devour one another, take heed that ye be not consumed one of another.** *This I say then, Walk in the Spirit, and ye shall not fulfil the lust of the flesh* (Galatians 5:13-16).

Throughout the history of the Church we have seen example after example of the "madness" that ensues when Christians turn on one another. We have little to fear from the world when we have such a propensity for shooting our own wounded.

The Inquisition and the Crusades are dark chapters in the history of the Church. Certain traditions had become so engrained in the fabric of Christianity, that murder and mayhem seemed to be a normal response to the issues of that day. Christian leaders chose *social and political chaos* rather than sacrifice their *sacred cows*.

The result: the Dark Ages, a time characterized by many of the same mad cow disease symptoms—pain, disorientation, confusion, imbalance, incontinence, and violence.

Time Will Tell

Second, note the long period of incubation that characterizes these diseases. The ill results of "*biting and devouring one another*" are not always immediately apparent, but time will tell. The tainted offspring of sacred cows may take generations to manifest themselves. It is all too true that the iniquity of the fathers is visited upon the children to the third and fourth generations. (See Exodus 34:7.)

Sometimes we are oh so conscious of the burden of tradition that our forefathers have bequeathed to us, yet our mask obstructs the view of the sacred cow ranch we are maintaining for our own children.

Practical May Not Be Proper

Third, the underlying reason for the outbreak of mad cow disease was that the natural order of things had been violated. It is not natural for a herbivore to be fed the diet of a carnivore.

It is no wonder that an epidemic would occur when meat-and-bone meal is made from diseased animals.

The farmers who resorted to this practice did so because they thought it would increase their production and thus their "bottom line." It seemed such a practical solution to the problem of maintaining profitability in the capricious agricultural industry.

But many times what is *practical* may not be *proper*. Later, I will share with you how God is a God of the practical; but remember, it is never at the expense of His principles.

The Bible story of King David transporting the Ark of the Covenant to Jerusalem is a case in point.

The Ark of the Covenant had not been in its proper place for many years. Long before the time of David, in fact, before Israel had a king at all, the elders of Israel conspired to use the Ark outside the scope of its sanctioned purpose.

The Israelites were at war with the Philistines, and had been defeated in a battle, losing four thousand of their fighting men. (See First Samuel 4:2.) The elders were disturbed over this event, but they remembered how Joshua had been instructed by God to send the Ark ahead of the people at the crossing of the Jordan River when the Israelites had first invaded the land of Canaan to conquer it. (See Joshua 3.) Surely this same technique would turn their tide of fortune in the current situation.

So they went to Shiloh where the Tabernacle had been for many years, and brought the Ark of the Covenant back to the battlefield. All the Israelites cheered the arrival of the Ark, and even the Philistines were frightened by all the hubbub.

But the strategy of the elders failed, for the next day Israel was once again defeated, this time losing 30 thousand men. To make matters even worse, the Philistines captured the Ark.

Now, an obvious lesson emerges from this event. Just because God sanctioned the use of the Ark in this manner in the past did not necessarily mean that such use was proper for the current situation. Rather than making their own decision to take the Ark into battle, the elders should have been seeking God's counsel in the situation. After all, the Ark was not a magical lucky charm that could guarantee success. It was Jehovah's presence and approval that would make Israel victorious, not resorting to a dark superstition.

The lesson? Never take all your cues from past experiences. Always seek a fresh word from the Lord.

Israel did not learn this lesson, as subsequent history reveals. The Ark remained with the Philistines for a very short while—just seven months. The fact that seven is God's perfect number didn't even help them. This coveted box brought them only misfortune and they decided to send it back to the Israelites.

The way they returned it is very interesting and pertinent to the rest of our story. (See First Samuel 6.)

They selected two milk cows with nursing calves and harnessed them to a cart on which they put the Ark. They penned up the two calves and turned the cows with the cart loose on the road. Their thinking was that the direction the cows started walking would be a sign regarding whether they had correctly connected their misfortune with the presence of the Ark in their land.

Sure enough, like a magnet drawn to a piece of steel the cows headed straight toward Beth Shemesh in Israelite territory. Now it was a minor miracle for these milk cows to abandon their calves and head up the road in the direction of the enemy. The natural thing would have been for them to linger in the area where their calves had been penned. For the cows to do otherwise was essentially supernatural.

Once the Ark was in Beth Shemesh, the men of that town decided to look inside the Ark. When they did, the Lord struck down 70 of them.[3] The people of Beth Shemesh cried out, *"Who is able to stand before this holy Lord God? And to whom shall it* [the Ark] *go up from us?"* (1 Sam. 6:20 NKJV).

Another lesson: unauthorized people had no business touching the Ark of the Covenant.

The men of neighboring Kirjath Jearim were petitioned to come over and take possession of the Ark, and it was transported it to the home of Abinadab. Here the Ark remained for 20 years.[4]

Fast forward through the reign of King Saul of Israel. Now David is king and has conquered the city of Jerusalem and has set out to make this city his capital and stronghold. One of his first decisions regarding the new seat of government was to bring the Ark to Jerusalem and eventually build a fine Temple in which to house it properly. Of course, it would not be until the reign of his son, Solomon, that the Temple would be built, but for David it was important to get the Ark to Jerusalem without delay.

With great fanfare and accompanied by an army of 30 thousand men, David set out for the home of Abinadab to retrieve the Ark of the Covenant. (See Second Samuel 6.)

The Bible does not say whose idea it was, but the decision was made to put the Ark on a new cart drawn by oxen. We might speculate that the idea came from the family of Abinadab. After all, they had personally experienced the return of the Ark from the Philistines and knew it had been transported as far as Beth Shemesh on a Philistine cart. They also knew the story of how the Philistines had used the milk cows as a sign from God that the Ark should be returned to Israel. No doubt, they had rehearsed the story, by the camp-fires, of how those milk cows had gone against their natural instincts and abandoned their calves to bring the Ark home to Israel.

If this method of transportation had worked for the Philistines, and had even been apparently used by God, then surely it would be the way for this current situation. Wrong!

The Ark was set on the cart and Abinadab's two sons, Uzzah and Ahio, walked with the oxen, driving them along. Apparently Ahio was walking ahead of the oxen and Uzzah was walking behind them near the cart.

It seemed like a fine plan. Everything was working great! Everybody was excited. The singers were singing. The musicians were playing. Even the king was participating in the festivities. This was a great day! The Ark was on its way to the new capital city.

But as they approached Nachon's threshing floor, something happened. Most Bible translations say that the oxen stumbled. The Hebrew translation actually says that the oxen jostled the cart. Whether they hit a bump in the road, they stumbled, they balked, or were just stupid oxen is really not the issue. Uzzah thought the Ark was about to fall and he reached out to steady it. It was the last thing he ever reached for. The Lord got mad and Uzzah got buried!

Lesson One—Never let the Ark be used in an unauthorized way.

Lesson Two—Never let unauthorized people touch the Ark.

David knew that the proper method for transporting the Ark was on the shoulders of the Levites. No matter how practical (convenient) the oxen cart method may have seemed, there was no justification for deviating from divine protocol. This newfound method proved not to be very "Uzzah friendly."

It didn't matter that this method had worked for the Philistines. It didn't matter that God apparently even led the Philistines' milk cows supernaturally. The bottom line was that the *practical* should never override the *proper*.

Uzzah died an unnecessary death. His family had to live with the grief of losing him. But Uzzah had only done what any person would have done under those circumstances. He had reached out to protect the Ark.

The people learned another lesson that day: God does not need our help, but He does demand our obedience.

The grand celebration died beside the oxcart that day at Nachon's threshing floor. The improper use of cows had delivered a severe penalty. Triumph had turned to tragedy.

The ark was taken to the nearby home of Obededom and left there until King David could regroup and make another attempt to bring the Ark to Jerusalem.

That day was a day of despair. "How shall the ark of the Lord come to me?" was David's fearful question. As he silently led the 30 thousand soldiers and all the singers and musicians back home, he must have wrestled with the doubt of ever fulfilling his dream of bringing the Ark to Jerusalem.

The message of this story is so obvious that it hardly needs elaboration, but perhaps some applications are in order.

Silk Purses and Sows' Ears

How often have we put our sacred cows to work in the Kingdom enterprise, thinking that we were "helping" God? How often have we borrowed the methods of the world, and tried to sanctify the unholy? We have ignored God's clearly stated principles, and attempted to do God's work our way. As they say where I come from, we are attempting to make silk purses out of sows' ears!

The purity of church government as it was practiced in the New Testament has never been duplicated since those days. The presbyterianism of modern times is a far cry from the multiplicity of ministry practiced by the apostles, and the episcopalian and congregational forms of modern church government have no New Testament counterparts at all. (When referring to presbyterianism and episcopalian, I am referencing forms of government, not denominations.)

Where did all these ecclesiastical variations come from? A study of church history reveals the origins date back to the second century. Shortly after the death of John, the last of the original 12 apostles, and the passing of the apostles' immediate successors, the church redefined some of its basic terminology. For instance, the Greek word for bishop[5] means "overseer," and was one of several biblical designations for the leaders of local congregations in the early church. In the second century, however, the role of the bishop was redefined to mean a leader with extra-local jurisdiction—in other words, a leader over many congregations in a region.

Where did this idea come from? It was copied from the form of government found at the time throughout the Roman Empire. The Caesar appointed governors over city-states. These rulers were based in metropolitan areas that included not only the city but the surrounding region as well. The rise of the office of bishop during this period was nothing more than the church copying the prevalent form of government of the day.

So what's wrong with that? The episcopalian form of church government reinstituted a hierarchical clergy along the lines of the Old Testament Aaronic priesthood. God's intent for Christianity was that it would be "...*a royal priesthood, an holy nation...*" (1 Peter 2:9). God desires direct communication with his covenant people. He does not want to communicate with them through a priest. Instead, He wants them all to be priests through whom He can communicate His message of reconciliation to the world.

When the episcopalian form of church government emerged in the second century, it created an unnecessary buffer between God and His people. It was a secular idea borrowed from the world that has proven, for centuries, to be a hindrance to the Kingdom.

In the Revelation, Jesus' message to the churches of Ephesus and Pergamos contained the warning that they were harboring a sect with whom He was greatly displeased—the Nicolaitans. (See Revelation 2:6,15.) Although scholars disagree as to exactly who these people were,[6] the meaning of the word itself sheds some light on the subject. It literally means "the domination of the people."[7] Whether this is the primary meaning of the ancient word *Nicolaitans* or not, the fact remains that God despises any system that suppresses His people and keeps them from being all He has destined them to be.

But what about the congregational form of church government? This idea emerged many centuries later during the time of the Protestant Reformation, and it too was a reflection of the time. Almost simultaneously with this religious revolution of the 16th century, there was a social and political revolution—

the Renaissance—that spanned the 14th to the 17th centuries, and marked the transition from the medieval to the modern world. It culminated with the American and French Revolutions in the 18th century and the introduction of widespread democracy throughout the developing world.

It should come as no surprise that as the people had an increasingly greater voice in their political governments, this trend would also show up in the churches. And it did, along with all the church politics, committees, and voting procedures with which we are so familiar today. This doesn't mean that procedures are all bad, unless the voice of the people becomes louder than the voice of God.

Modern presbyterianism, though it pays lip service to the eldership form of government found in the Scriptures, is, as we have said, a far cry from the pure practices of the New Testament churches. Today, there is little difference between the elder boards of presbyterian government based churches and the deacon boards of numerous other denominational churches.

Have I offended a sacred cow in your neighborhood?

Why does Christian music follow the trends of the day? Why couldn't there have been "rap" in the Church before it was developed in the world? Why does the Church seem to be composed of followers instead of trendsetters? There was a time when the Church set the pace in music, architecture, sculpture, painting, and literature. How long has it been since the world took its cue from anything the Church is doing?

Today the Church follows the fads of the world, only we are usually about a decade behind the times. Just about the time we catch up to what is "in," the world has moved on and we find ourselves scrambling to catch up to where they were.

No wonder the world largely dismisses the Church as irrelevant. They look at us and see us doing the same things that they were doing last month or last year or ten years ago.

Jesus Himself said, *"The children of this world are in their generation wiser than the children of light"* (Luke 16:8b).

The Church in America has spent the last decades taking pride in its spasmodic, knee-jerk reactions to current trends—prayer taken out of the public schools, the Ten Commandments removed from courthouses, gay rights and homosexual marriage, the proliferation of abortion. Instead we should feel ashamed that we have not been proactively setting the agenda in our governments, our schools, our military, our courts, and in the media and the marketplace.

We have borrowed Philistine cows to carry the sacred vessels of the Lord. Is it any wonder that there is death all around the oxcart and confusion and despair in the camp?

Even among ourselves, we are sometimes so devoid of scriptural understanding and revelational direction that we trek by the busload to the faraway places of the world hoping against hope that we will find some innovation we can carry back home to try to duplicate.

The innovations that we need, however, will come only when there is a fresh urgency to immerse ourselves in God's Word and to seek *His* face for a direct revelation from the heavenlies. Then and only then will we see the kind of sovereign moves of God that will bring the Ark to Jerusalem.

Chariot Chasing and Shadow Casting

Years ago the bus ministry movement was instrumental in growing numerous churches across America. During that time, I remember someone saying of our "follow-the-fad" tendencies, "If the leaders of the early New Testament Church had operated the way we do today, then immediately after Philip was used by God in the conversion of the Ethiopian eunuch, there would have been chariot-chasing seminars popping up all over Judea."

Do you think that any of the other leaders in the New Testament tried to come up with ways they could enhance their shadows after they saw the people clamoring to get into position so Peter's shadow would fall on them? I don't think so.

As far as we know, Paul never taught anyone else how to shake off snakes and John never gave lessons on island-based hallucinations. No, the new leaders relied on their personal relationship with God to touch people's lives, and became known as the ones who "*...turned the world upside down...*" (Acts 17:6).

It is high time that we learn to be creators, not duplicators—to be entrepreneurs, not consumers. We must learn to take center stage and stop hanging around in the backstage shadows like a bunch of religious groupies. We must reverse the trend of the mad cows and the Philistine cows and the sacred cows by devoting ourselves anew to following the divine protocol of the saving Lamb.

If the bloodied Lamb does not saturate us, the mad cows will destroy us!

Endnotes

1. The names in this story are fictitious—the incidents are real. To read more first-hand accounts of Creutzfeldt-Jakob disease victims, visit http://

www.hbsef.org/personal.htm. It is with respect for the victims and their families that I cite these instances. I pray for the day when both the physical and the spiritual diseases are cured.

2. http://science.howstuffworks.com/mad-cow-disease1.htm.

3. The King James Version says that "fifty thousand and seventy men" were killed. The NAV, NIV, NRSV, and NLT say that 70 were killed. These translations are based on a few medieval Hebrew manuscripts that omit the words for "fifty thousand." Even though the textual evidence favors the higher number, the smaller number seems more reasonable.

4. First Samuel 7:2 says that the Ark remained at Abinadab's house for 20 years. Yet it was placed there before Saul was anointed king and remained there until during the reign of King David. Acts 13:21 states that Saul reigned for 40 years. At any rate, the Ark was at Abinadab's house a long time!

5. Bishop—Greek *episcope*, (Strong's #1984). From the root words eip (Strong's #1909) which means "over" and *skopos* (Strong's #4649) from which we get our English word "scope," the base of which, *skeptomai*, means "to inspect, to look, to see." Thus the word bishop literally and simply means "overseer." The English word *episcopal* is from the Greek word episcope.

6. Some scholars believe these were the follows of the heretic Nicolaus. Others think the name indicates their doctrine, that of a hierarchical clergy. (See next note.)

7. The Greek word *Nikolaites* (Strong's #3531) comes from two Greek roots. Nikos (Strong's #3534) means "to conquer," from which the modern brand name

Nike™ derives. Laos (Strong's #2992) means "the people," from which we get the English word "laity." Thus the word *Nicolaitans* literally means "the conquering of the people."

Epigraph

Every business organization should have a vice-president in charge of constant renewal.

—*Dwayne Orton*

None are so old as those who have outlived enthusiasm.

—*Henry David Thoreau*

Notes

_____

_____

_____

_____

_____

_____

_____

_____

_____

_____

_____

_____

_____

_____

_____

_____

_____

_____

_____

_____

_____

CHAPTER 6

Cow Killing

"A Picture of Worship"

MARK Twain said, "If you put a cat on a hot stove he'll never sit on a hot stove again. In fact he'll never sit on any stove!"

When it came to the Ark, King David had spent some time on a hot stove, so to speak. So this time he took every precaution to ensure that his second attempt to bring the Ark of the Covenant to Jerusalem did not end in another fiasco. No doubt much soul-searching preceded his next effort, but one thing is certain—he was determined not to rely on unsanctioned methods to get the job done.

David was not overly impatient to proceed. He waited three months before making another attempt. Great blessings had come to Obed-Edom's home because the Ark had been left there, and only after hearing this good report did David overcome his fear of dealing with the Ark.

This time the Ark was successfully brought to Jerusalem in parade form amid great rejoicing and fanfare.

And it was told king David, saying, The Lord hath blessed the house of Obededom, and all that pertaineth unto him, because of the ark of God. So David went and brought up the ark of God from the house of Obededom into the city of David with gladness. And it was so, that when they that bare the ark of the Lord had gone six paces, he sacrificed oxen and fatlings. And David danced before the Lord with all his might; and David was girded with a linen ephod. So David and all the house of Israel brought up the ark of the Lord with shouting, and with the sound of the trumpet (2 Samuel 6:12-15).

But what was the difference between this second attempt and the first?

Done the Right Way

First of all, the Ark was transported in the prescribed manner—on the shoulders of the Levites as Moses had commanded. David decreed, *"None ought to carry the ark of God but the Levites: for them hath the Lord chosen to carry the ark of God, and to minister unto Him for ever"* (1 Chron. 15:2).

Acknowledging God's prescribed order—doing what was *proper* instead of what was *practical*—was one of the key ingredients that led to David's success this time. No Philistine cow-and-cart method was allowed to corrupt the orderly procession to the holy city.

And yet our emphasis should not be on methodology alone. The real secret to David's success was that finally he was truly acknowledging God—His ways, His will, and His Word.

Although there had been a lot of fanfare surrounding the first attempt to bring the Ark to Jerusalem, missing was the acknowledgment that God's pleasure must come first. He is much more concerned with obedience than with fanfare—even when we mistake that fanfare for worship.

Real Worship Was Present

That brings us to the *second* important difference between the successful attempt and the first failed attempt—real worship was present.

Once the Ark had been lifted to the shoulders of the Levites and they had walked six paces, David stopped the procession and ordered the sacrifice of an ox and a fatted calf. At this earliest opportunity, as soon as he could discern that there was not going to be another wrath of God incident, he delayed the journey and took time to acknowledge God in an unmistakable way—with a burnt offering, a blood sacrifice.

Scholars are divided over exactly what this statement about the six paces and the sacrifices in the story means. Some think that every six paces, the procession stopped to offer another couplet of a bull and a calf. Others propose that the procession did not stop, but that in its wake at a distance of every six paces two additional animals were sacrificed.

If either of these scenarios were true, then an aerial view of the journey from Obed-Edom's house to Jerusalem would depict a ten-mile trail of blood and smoke. I must tell you and I think you'll agree, worship is a journey and not an event.

Old Testament commentators Keil and Delitzsch have offered the observation:

These words are generally understood as meaning that sacrifices of this kind were offered along the whole way, at the distance of six paces apart. This would certainly have been a possible thing, and...even the immense number of sacrificial animals that would have been required is no valid objection to such an assumption.[1]

Worship was a missing element in David's first attempt, but it plays a significant role in the success of the second.

At this point David could have easily rejoiced in singing one of our current worship songs, "I'm coming back to the heart of worship, and it's all about You, Lord, it's all about You!"[2]

Worship—expressed through *obedience* and *sacrifice*—is what this story is really all about!

Sacred cows and mad cows can kill! We've already seen that.

But how do you kill the sacred cows? The answer is so simple that it is overlooked in our quest for admission to the "deeper life" club. The answer is nothing more—and certainly nothing less—than *worship*!

In addition to the sacrifices that were made that day, David demonstrated an enthusiasm and a commitment that had not previously been seen in his life. David had always been a worshiper. He was known as *"the sweet psalmist of Israel."*[3] But on this day, he laid aside his royal garments and *"danced before the Lord with all his might."* He danced for ten miles all the way to Jerusalem!

When the procession arrived at Jerusalem, David's wife, Michal, was looking from her window in the royal palace and was embarrassed by David's energetic display and by the fact that he was clothed only in his undergarments. The Bible says, "*...she despised him in her heart*" (2 Sam. 6:16).

When she later chided David for his behavior, he was undeterred in his conviction that his blatant expression of worship was justified. David said to Michal, "*It was before the Lord, which chose me before thy father, and before all his house, to appoint me ruler over the people of the Lord, over Israel: therefore will I play before the Lord. And I will yet be more vile than thus, and will be base in mine own sight*" (2 Sam. 6:21-22a). In other words, "Honey, I did this for nobody but the Lord, and you ain't seen nothin' yet!"

Second Samuel chapter 6 ends with the sad implication that because Michal ridiculed David, her womb dried up. Anyone who ridicules true worship will be barren; they run the risk of becoming unfruitful.

If I were to show you a picture of worship I'd show you Calvary—an intersection where vertical and horizontal beams come together on top of a lonely hill, where God gets as close to man as man can handle. Humanity and divinity become so intertwined, it's difficult to tell them apart. One moment you hear words of divinity, "*Father, forgive them*" and the next moment words of humanity, "*My God, My God, why have You forsaken Me?*"[4] When we see the picture of Calvary, amazingly we see two worlds—ecstasy and reality. One is His; the other is ours. Worship allows us to experience them both.

There are more parallels than you can imagine between Calvary and David's act of worship. They become obvious as we study these stories side by side. At least four common elements capture our attention.

Cows and Commitment

First, in both instances there is *sacrifice*.

Calvary is not one-dimensional. There are many ways to understand the sacrifice made there. Doctrinally, we use words like propitiation, atonement, and justification. Seldom do we equate Calvary with worship—but that is essentially what it is.

All the bulls and goats and lambs and turtledoves and pigeons of the Old Testament sacrificial system were offered as acts of worship to God. There were other aspects as well, as seen in the different names for these sacrifices—peace offerings, transgress offerings, wave offerings. But they all are acknowledgments of God's place of sovereignty and of humankind's place of dependence on Him. That makes all of these Old Testament sacrifices a form of worship.

Jesus came and was declared by John the Baptist to be *"the Lamb of God, which taketh away the sin of the world"* (John 1:29b). If indeed all the Old Testament sacrifices are acts of worship, then Jesus as the ultimate sacrificial Lamb is the ultimate expression of worship.

David knew the value of blood sacrifice, and on this occasion he was determined not to rely on pomp and circumstance to carry the day. In addition to the singers and musicians, he brought along animals to be sacrificed to the Lord.

We, of course, no longer need animal sacrifices since the ultimate Sacrifice has been offered. But in our deepest, most intense moments of worship, we know the blood still flows.

Jesus instructed His disciples on His last night with them when...

He took the cup, and gave thanks, and said, Take this, and divide it among yourselves: For I say unto you, I will not drink of the fruit of the vine, until the kingdom of God shall come. And He took bread, and gave thanks, and brake it, and gave unto them, saying, This is My body which is given for you: this do in remembrance of Me. Likewise also the cup after supper, saying, This cup is the new testament in My blood, which is shed for you (Luke 22:17-20).

Paul, the apostle, recounted this experience and set the pattern for us to continue the practice of celebrating the Lord's Supper in perpetuity. He summed up the essence of this practice by saying, *"For as often as ye eat this bread, and drink this cup, ye do show the Lord's death till He come"* (1 Cor. 11:26).

Not only the partaking in the Lord's Supper, but all our acts of worship are blood bought.

Worship goes far beyond singing and prayers. Worship should occur in everything we do. It has more to do with lifestyle than with particular activities.

Paul admonished the Roman believers: *"Therefore, I urge you, brothers, in view of God's mercy, to **offer** your bodies as living sacrifices, holy and **pleasing to God**—this is your spiritual act of worship"* (Rom. 12:1 NIV).

Notice in this verse that an offering preludes the phrase "pleasing to God." It's impossible to please the Lord without worship and it's impossible to worship without an offering. Ultimately our entire lives become an offering to the Lord—*"a living sacrifice, holy and pleasing to God."*

Proper Is More Important Than Practical

Second, in both instances there was *submission.*

Jesus prayed in the Garden of Gethsemane, *"Father, if Thou be willing, remove this cup from Me: nevertheless not My will, but Thine, be done"* (Luke 22:42). Then He stretched His arms out in submission to receive the nails.

Before Him, David, too, after months of seeking, realized that his only option, if he ever intended to successfully bring the Ark to Jerusalem, was to pray, "Not my will, but Yours, Lord!"

Even though his desire to bring the Ark to Jerusalem was right on target as far as the will of God was concerned, David's experience vividly demonstrates that all too often we commandeer the things of God and corrupt them with our own ambitions. We want to do *God's will,* but we want to do it *our way!*

But God is not satisfied until we totally surrender everything to Him. He is not glorified when we become so enamored with the trappings of the Kingdom that we forget the King!

How often do we speak of *our* ministries, *our* churches, *our* callings, and forget that it's really all about Him! I hear people say they are having a bad day. How can you have a bad day when it's "the day the Lord has made"?

Worship is, at its core, submission to God. If our singing, our hand clapping, our dancing are not motivated by submission, they're just racket and motion. David's first attempt to transport the Ark was accompanied by singers and musicians, but obedience and submission were missing.

When he made his second attempt, the singers and the musicians were there again, but the result was not just clamor and chaos—it was harmony and order and personal involvement by David the king.

Liberty Is Quite Clear

Third, in both instances there was *transparency*.

Jesus was stripped of His clothing at Calvary and hung naked, exposed, and helpless in front of the whole world. It was to this extreme that His submission to the Father took Him.

David, too, found it appropriate to undress before the multitude that day, and dance with abandonment in his expression of submission to God. Just maybe the reason he was called a "man after God's own heart" was because he never tried to hide his heart. A mask would never cover something so obvious.

How much more dignified it would have been to have kept on his trappings of royalty. To lead the procession in a regal and stately fashion would have been much more in keeping with his position and authority. Certainly Michal would have been more comfortable when he arrived in town if he had his clothes on.

Michal had not participated in the event. Was she aware of David's dark moments following his first embarrassing attempt to move the Ark? Did she know that David had already lost his dignity in that first fiasco? He thought that nothing more could be lost. Unlike his wife, David thought about how much better it would be to cast aside the royal façade and be honest and open before God.

Worship requires transparency. If we attempt to fool God with our mask of self-righteousness, He sees right through it. Our veils do not fool God, but they do create a barrier between Him and us.

Jesus told the story of two men praying in the Temple:

Two men went up into the temple to pray; the one a Pharisee, and the other a publican. The Pharisee stood and prayed thus with himself, God, I thank Thee, that I am not as other men are, extortioners, unjust, adulterers, or even as this publican. I fast twice in the week, I give tithes of all that I possess. And the publican, standing afar off, would not lift up so much as his eyes unto heaven, but smote upon his breast, saying, God be merciful to me a sinner. I tell you, this man went down to his house justified rather than the other: for every one that exalteth himself shall be abased; and he that humbleth him-self shall be exalted (Luke 18:10-14).

The irony in this story is startling. Our efforts to impress God produce exactly the opposite results. But when we hum-ble ourselves before Him in transparency, even the grossest of evils are forgiven and we find ourselves *"accepted in the beloved"* (Eph. 1:6b).

David discovered this secret, and it is reflected throughout the Psalms:

The Lord is nigh unto them that are of a broken heart; and saveth such as be of a contrite spirit (Psalm 34:18).

The sacrifices of God are a broken spirit: a broken and a contrite heart, O God, Thou wilt not despise (Psalm 51:17).

Sometimes to make ourselves available to God to this extent will bring us ridicule and derision. Jesus experienced that; David did too. But in the end we have to ask ourselves, Which is more important: impressing people or impressing God?

In Jesus' day there were many "secret disciples." They knew the teachings of Christ were true, but they could not bring themselves to make a public profession of faith because they feared the Jewish authorities. But Jesus said, "*Whosoever therefore shall be ashamed of Me and of My words in this adulterous and sinful generation; of him also shall the Son of man be ashamed, when He cometh in the glory of His Father with the holy angels*" (Mark 8:38).

There is a liberty that comes only when we are transparent before God. Apostle Paul described the veil that Moses put over his face as being an impediment to the Israelites developing a true relationship with God.

Seeing then that we have such hope, we use great plainness of speech: and not as Moses, which put a veil over his face, that the children of Israel could not stedfastly look to the end of that which is abolished: but their minds were blinded: for until this day remaineth the same veil untaken away in the reading of the old testament; which veil is done away in Christ. But even unto this day, when Moses is read, the veil is upon their heart (2 Corinthians 3:12-15).

Paul's point: even though Moses' veil had originally served a practical purpose—that of protecting the people from the brightness of his face when he came down from Mount Sinai—once the brightness faded, the veil was no longer necessary. But Moses refused to discard it, and consequently created a barrier between God and His people. In Paul's own day, he declared that the veil was still over their hearts.

But, he went on to explain, if the veil could be taken away, the results would be most positive and wondrous.

> *Nevertheless when it shall turn to the Lord, the veil shall be taken away. Now the Lord is that Spirit: and where the Spirit of the Lord is, there is **liberty**. But we all, with open face beholding as in a glass the glory of the Lord, are changed into the same image from glory to glory, even as by the Spirit of the Lord* (2 Corinthians 3:16-18).

When we get rid of our veils and get out from behind the masks, the result is clearly liberty and transformation from glory to glory. This leads us to our last comparison of Calvary and David's moving of the Ark to Jerusalem.

It's Time to Dance

Fourth, in both instances there was *joy*.

For Jesus the joy was not outwardly apparent. The scene at Calvary was dark and foreboding. There was gore, not glory, at least to the uninformed observer.

But Paul, the writer of the Epistle to the Hebrews, had a deeper spiritual insight. He declared, *"Looking unto Jesus the* author and finisher of our faith; who for the joy that was set before Him endured the cross, despising the shame..." (Heb. 12:2).

Jesus' attitude was further described by the writer to the Hebrews by quoting an Old Testament Messianic passage in Psalm 40: *"Then said I, Lo, I come (in the volume of the book it is written of Me,) to do Thy will, O God"* (Heb. 10:7).

Over and over Jesus declared that He had not come to this planet to do His own will.

"My meat is to do the will of Him that sent Me, and to finish His work" (John 4:34).

"I seek not Mine own glory..." (John 8:50).

"I must work the works of Him that sent Me..." (John 9:4).

"For I have not spoken of Myself; but the Father which sent Me, He gave Me a commandment, what I should say, and what I should speak" (John 12:49).

Jesus' delight was to do the will of the Father. The Father's will was that Jesus would go to the Cross. This was the *"joy that was set before Him"* that enabled Him to *"endure the Cross"* even while He was *"despising the shame."*

David, in a similar fashion, disregarded the contempt he would be subjected to in order to experience the joy of worship.

When he saw, after just six paces, that the journey was going to be successful, he stopped the procession to give honor to God. The transporting of the Ark became secondary to that which was more important—worship. He then danced all the way to town. There was joy in the camp. The exhilaration, the elation, the ecstasy of worship flavored everything that was done that day.

But, what exactly is worship? Is it singing and shouting? Is it clapping hands and dancing feet? Is it ceremony and processions?

Three words merit attention—"praise," "glory," and "worship."

Three times in the first chapter of his Epistle to the Ephesians Paul used the phrase *"to the praise of his glory"* (see Eph. 1:6,12,14). We use these words quite often in Christian circles, but what do they actually mean?

The word *praise* derives from a Greek word that means "to tell a story that commends another."[5] In other words, exclaiming, "Praise the Lord!" in a church worship service is not the truest expression of the word "praise." But when on the street the next day, we encounter someone and begin a conversation with something like, "Let me tell you what the Lord has done for me..."—that is praise in its highest form. It is not so much the words we say to God as much as the words we say *about* God that constitutes true praise.

Praise is *adoration*, but it is also *testimony*. The overcomers in the Revelation did so *"...by the blood of the Lamb, and by the word of their testimony"* (Rev. 12:11a). We have already seen how the blood of sacrifice enables one to achieve success, just as David's story demonstrated. The "word of testimony" works in tandem with the blood to achieve that end as well. All the way from Obed-Edom's house to Jerusalem, David and his people were worshiping God, and that worship buoyed them to victory.

Our praise, not only in the *sanctuary* but also in the *streets*, is a driving force, a dynamic lifestyle that propels us into a deeper life of achievement and fruitfulness. When we realize the journey is more valuable than the gesture, we begin to understand worship.

To God Be the Glory

The word *glory* is another word that we frequently bandy about in our "church-speak." "Glory to God!" "Wasn't that a glorious service!" "The choir sang and the glory fell!"

But what is "glory," biblically? The word *glory* means, "that which has weight."[6] The picture that comes to mind is one of a set of scales in the marketplace. The side of the scales that dips down indicates that the contents of that side are more valuable.

So when we use the word *glory* with respect to worship, we are talking about anything that demonstrates God's "weight" or value. The truth is He always tips the scales. Glory be to God! This is the essence of the phrase we find repeated in the Revelation about worth or worthiness.

Thou art worthy, O Lord, to receive glory and honour and power: for Thou hast created all things, and for Thy pleasure they are and were created (Revelation 4:11).

And they sung a new song, saying, Thou art worthy to take the book, and to open the seals thereof: for Thou wast slain, and hast redeemed us to God by Thy blood out of every kindred, and tongue, and people, and nation (Revelation 5:9).

...Worthy is the Lamb that was slain to receive power, and riches, and wisdom, and strength, and honour, and glory, and blessing (Revelation 5:12).

Even God's people, when found to be honorable, are spoken of using this same term.

Thou hast a few names even in Sardis which have not defiled their garments; and they shall walk with Me in white: for they are worthy (Revelation 3:4).

What is at issue here? When something has immense value, we can readily ascribe to it the word *glory*.

Everything we say or do that demonstrates God's inestimable worth is an action that brings "glory" to Him. Paul admonished, "*whatsoever ye do, do all to the glory of God*" (1 Cor. 10:31b).

This was the concept that motivated the early Amish furniture makers in their craft. They often would finish the backs and insides of furniture, such as a chest of drawers, to the same high gloss finish as the outsides, fronts, and tops. Many times they were questioned about the practicality of their techniques: "Why do you waste time and material finishing those parts that few if anyone will ever see?"

Their reply was quite telling: "There is One who always sees. This piece of furniture was not really built for the customer—it was built for Him."

This is called "playing to an audience of One." How often do we consider the mundane activities of everyday life to be acts of worship? They can be if we determine to do them in such a way that brings glory to His Name. I have a strong feeling that our customers and employers would also find greater satisfaction in our work if we followed this principle. Shoddy workmanship and negligent practices would not be tolerated if our guiding principle was pleasing God in all things, and letting all things become an act of worship.

A Lesson From a Dog

Consider the word *worship*. The etymology of words is many times a field of delightful discovery. Who would ever think that the Greek word for worship comes from a root word that means "dog"?[7] But that is exactly its origin!

The Greek word means "to fawn" or "to prostrate oneself in homage." It literally paints the picture of a dog approaching its master in a crouch, preparing to lick his hand. I never thought my big brown Labrador retriever could teach me such a spiritual lesson. I thought he just liked the taste of my hand. What an honor to discover—my dog worships me!

The antiquated word *fawn* carries this same connotation. It means "in humans, to seek notice or favor by servile behavior" or "in dogs, to behave affectionately."

Worship, then, can be understood as "submissive reverence; obedient devotion; deferential regard."

Another picture of worship found in Scripture illustrates this definition beautifully:

Then Jesus six days before the passover came to Bethany, where Lazarus was which had been dead, whom He raised from the dead. There they made Him a supper; and Martha served: but Lazarus was one of them that sat at the table with Him. Then took Mary a pound of ointment of spikenard, very costly, and anointed the feet of Jesus, and wiped His feet with her hair: and the house was filled with the odour of the ointment. Then saith one of His disciples, Judas Iscariot, Simon's son, which should betray Him, Why was not this ointment sold for three hundred pence, and given to the poor? This he said, not that he cared for the poor; but because he was a thief, and had the bag, and bare what was put therein. Then said Jesus, Let her alone: against the day of My burying hath she kept this. For the poor always ye have with you; but Me ye have not always (John 12:1-8).

We would not be denigrating Mary to compare her actions toward the Lord with that of a dog licking its master's hand. Such devotion will always be contemptible to those who do not understand its essence, just as David's dance was not appreciated by Michal.

There will always be those who view such devotion as a waste of valuable energy or resources. But God's response will always remain, "Leave these people alone. I honor what they are doing for Me."

Jesus offered the additional insight that Mary worshiped Him this way because she had an understanding, a premonition, if you will, of His impending death. *"Against the day of My burying hath she kept this,"* He said.

It seems that Mary had caught a vision of Calvary and instinctively knew that it all was directly related to worship. No wonder she fell at His feet and wept. No wonder she lavished a precious ointment worth an entire year's wage on His feet.

There is also no wonder that no one else did what Mary did, and that Judas was even critical of her actions. They simply did not or could not see what Mary saw. Like Mary, our level of worship is predicated on our level of revelation.

When we fully realize the magnitude of that worship scene on Golgotha's hill, there is no telling what we will find ourselves doing in response. One thing is certain, however—preserving sacred cows won't be on the agenda. Like David, we won't be hitching them to our wagon—we'll be slaying them...every six steps if necessary.

David *returned God's Ark to its **proper** place.*

Christ at Calvary, through the ripping of the veil in the Temple, *released God's atonement into **every** place.*

We, through a lifestyle of true worship, can *restore God's authority* to **any** place.

When Jesus encountered the woman at Jacob's well in Samaria, she tried to deflect the conversation away from His *revelatory disclosure* concerning her past life by engaging Him in a *religious debate.* "Our forefathers," she said, "instructed us to worship on Mount Gerizim. You Jews insist on Mount Zion. How can anybody tell which way is right?"

Jesus' reply diverted her attention from geography to the true "heart of worship."

> *Woman, believe me, the hour cometh, when ye shall neither in this mountain, nor yet at Jerusalem, worship the Father. Ye worship ye know not what: we know what we worship: for salvation is of the Jews. But the hour cometh, and now is, when the true worshippers shall worship the Father in spirit and in truth: for the Father seeketh such to worship Him. God is a Spirit: and they that worship Him must worship Him in spirit and in truth* (John 4:21-24).

True worship, according to Jesus, has nothing to do with *outward form*, such as making a pilgrimage to one place or another. Rather, it has everything to do with *inward faith*, that is, worshiping God "*in spirit and in truth.*"

Worship is the highest function of the human spirit. The first four of the Ten Commandments warn against humans doing as they please regarding God and worship. Humans have more than *existence*; they have *essence*. For that reason their attitude toward God and their response in true worship is vitally important.

Our correct response to God is predicated on understanding who He is and who we are. The root of all our troubles is found in our creating gods of our own making and getting things out of their proper order.

> *Wherefore God also gave them up to uncleanness through the lusts of their own hearts, to dishonour their own bodies between themselves: Who changed the truth of God into a lie, and worshipped and*

served the creature more than the Creator, who is blessed for ever. Amen (Romans 1:24-25).

When we pervert worship by elevating the creature over the Creator, the results we can expect are "uncleanness" and "dishonor."

When true worship exists:

- God's glory will be revealed.

- God's forgiveness will be received.

- God's presence will be realized.

- God's power will be released.

Don't sell the farm—just kill the cows. David killed a cow every 18 feet. When he destroyed the cause of death and disorder, God brought about life and order. This may seem like an overkill (pun intended), but it teaches us the value of a constant worship lifestyle. Not a one-time event, but an epoch. Worship is not a *destination*, whether it is Jerusalem in David's case, or Heaven for us. Instead, it's a *journey*. It's what we should and need to do all along the way to our destination.

When one bends beneath the crimson flow, he assumes a true posture for worship. The blood of Christ and the bowing down of humanity must never be separated. There can be no dance without demolition. The good news is that *through* and *in* the Body of Christ there is a glorious congruency. The demolition and the dance literally come together. We dance not in the light of ritual and religion but in redemption and restoration.

Worship provides the ultimate way to re-member the Body. (See Hebrews 9:9-24.)

Endnotes

1. Keil & Delitzsch Commentary on the Old Testament: New Updated Edition, Electronic Database, 1996 by Hendrickson Publishers, Inc.

2. Matt Redman, "The Heart of Worship," *Blessed Be Your Name*, Vol. 1., 2005.

3. See Second Samuel 23:1.

4. See Luke 23:34; Matthew 27:46; Mark 15:34.

5. The word *praise* is translated from the Greek word *epainos* (Strong's #1868), which means "concretely, a commendable thing." It comes from two root words: *epi* (Strong's #1909), a general preposition that can be translated "toward" (among other possible words) and *ainos* (Strong's #136), which properly means "a story." Thus *epainos* means "to tell a story toward another" or "to tell a story for the benefit of another" or "to tell a story that commends another."

6. The word *glory* is translated from the Greek word *doxa* (Strong's #1391) and means "honor" or "dignity." In the Old Testament the word *glory* is translated from the Hebrew word *kabowd* (Strong's #3519) and is somewhat more enlightening. Because the translators of the Septuagint used the word *doxa* when translating the Old Testament word *kabowd* into Greek, we can be assured that these are synonymous words. *Kabowd* means "that which has weight" or "something heavy."

7. The word *worship* is translated from the Greek word *proskuneo* (Strong's #4352), which in turn derives from two root words: *pros* (Strong's #4314), which is a preposition of direction meaning "toward," and *kuon* (Strong's #2965), which means "dog."

Epigraph

I beseech you therefore, brethren, by the mercies of God, that you present your bodies a living sacrifice, holy, acceptable to God, which is your reasonable service (Romans 12:1 NKJV).

Watching from the window will never substitute for dancing in the parade.

—*Mark Briggs*

Job in his distraught condition sat in ashes and scraped himself with broken pottery (see Job 2:8). In order for there to be ashes, there must have been some previous sacrifices made. Job teaches us that worship *prior* to the trip always leaves a perfect trail for the humble spirit to follow.

—*Mark Briggs*

Notes

CHAPTER 7

Cows That Are OK

"Supports of Worship—Not Objects of Worship"

THE newlyweds were preparing for one of their first meals at home together and the new husband was just about to slide the roast into the oven. "Wait a minute, Babe," the new wife exclaimed, "that's not ready to cook yet!"

"Why not?" he replied. "I've already basted it and seasoned it just like you told me."

"But you haven't cut the end off yet."

"Whaddayumean?"

"Just cut about three or four inches off that smaller end and lay it sideways in the pan."

"But, why?"

"Because that's how my mother taught me to do it, and she never made a bad roast in her life."

"Okay, but why?"

"I don't know...that's just how it's done!"

"OK, OK," he said, setting the pan back on the counter and beginning to cut the end off the roast. "But I still don't get it. What's the purpose of this?"

"Listen," she insisted, "I've helped my mother prepare hundreds of roasts over the years, and we always did it this way. Just you wait and see...this will be the greatest roast beef you ever put in your mouth."

"Maybe so," he muttered, "but I intend to find out from your mom what this is all about!"

The roast beef turned out to be quite delicious, just as predicted; but later in the week,

when they were visiting her parents, the new husband asked his mother-in-law about the roast. "By the way, Mom," he said, "what's the big deal about cutting off the end of a roast before cooking it?"

"What are you talking about?" she wanted to know.

"You know, Mother," the new bride jumped in, "when you cook a roast, you always cut a couple of inches off one end and lay it alongside the rest of the roast. I helped you prepare many a roast, and we have always done it that way!"

The mother began to laugh hilariously. "Oh silly, when all you kids were at home, I never had a pan long enough for the size roasts that I needed to cook, so I cut the end off so it would fit in the pan!"

I wonder how many church traditions that once had a useful purpose are still being practiced long after they ceased to be necessary. Yet in true "calf-path" fashion, we dutifully continue to plod in that direction, many times no longer even knowing why we are doing it or what its original purpose was.

A Sacred Cow and a Silly Mouse

The typeface of the text you are reading right now is called a "font." Where did that word come from?

The earliest known printed books were produced using wooden blocks with the text carved on them. That, in turn, was then used as a printing plate. By the middle of the 15th century movable type had been invented in Europe. Movable type was also called foundry type or hot type. In foundry type, each piece of type was cast into a precise size from an alloy of lead. Each individual piece contained a raised image of a single letter, number, or other character. The block of metal that carried the raised image was called the "body." The raised image that was inked for printing was called the "face"—from this we got the term "typeface." Because these characters were formed from molten metal using a foundry process, they were also called "fonts."

Furthermore, the amount of space from baseline to baseline of "body" copy is called "leading," because in making up the page of type the compositors would use thin strips of lead to separate the lines of movable characters.

It has been several generations since type has been commercially cast in hot lead. The text you are reading about a printing industry sacred cow was digitally composed on a personal computer and was maneuvered on a screen by a "silly mouse." Although the historical "font" and "leading" cows remain in current usage in the publishing industry, no doubt one day even my own beloved plastic mouse will double-click its way down the "calf-path."

From Nags to Nukes

The United States' standard gauge railroad track is 4 feet, 8½ half inches wide. Where did such an unusual railway width come from? The English railroad-builders who came to America made the American railroad tracks the same width as were used in Great Britain. But where did the English come up with this peculiar width? The first British rail lines were built using the same gauge as the pre-railroad tramways that used horse-drawn wagons. The workmen who built the tramways used the same jigs and tools to build the new railways, so the simplest thing was to retain the standard wagon-wheel spacing.

Actually, though, the tradition has its original roots in a much earlier time—when Britain was part of the Roman Empire. The Roman legions comprised the greatest war machine known to mankind up until that time. One of its secrets of success was its mechanized efficiency—an efficiency based on standardized weapons, including the Roman war chariots that used a standard spacing between their wheels. The Roman standard was derived after trial-and-error efforts of early wagon and chariot builders. They determined the best width that would accommodate two horses' rear ends was the equivalent of 4 feet, 8½ inches, in our British-American traditional system of measurements.

Over time, the extensive Roman road network throughout the empire became deep ruts spaced exactly 4 feet, 8½ inches wide. If British wheel spacing didn't match the Roman ruts, the wheels would break. Thus the United States standard railroad gauge is a hand-me-down standard based on the original specification for an imperial Roman war chariot—illustrating perfectly why an already decided rut, in many cases, is the easy way to do things.

But the tradition doesn't end with the railroad tracks. The two big solid-fuel booster rockets (SRBs) attached to the sides of the main fuel tank that lifts the space shuttle into orbit are shipped from a Utah factory to the Florida launch site via train. The railroad from the factory runs through mountain tunnels only slightly wider than the standard gauge railroad track. Even if NASA's engineers wanted wider SRBs, the railway gauge limits their design and size. Modern American space shuttle design is bridled by ancient Roman horses' hind parts. What a story—from nags to nukes! Who would have ever dreamed with today's finest aerospace technology that the BTUs of our SRBs would be determined by two old grey mares' BUTTs!

But here is the important question. Does it really matter one way or the other? If the 4 foot, 8½ inch standard width works, why change it? Two innocent old nags can't be all that bad. If we decided to discontinue calling a typeface a "font," what better name could we come up with? If the roast comes out of the oven smelling and tasting great, what difference does it make if the piping hot serving for us was carved pre- or post-oven?

The Running of the Bulls

In understanding the concept of sacred cows, we must realize that there is nothing inherently good or bad about cows. It's the use we make of them and our attitude toward them that make the difference.

Every year, Spain holds the phenomenon of the running of the bulls. The scene appears to be one of an entire herd of crazed animals maliciously chasing and trying to gore the many helpless humans foolish enough to enter the streets at

BEHIND THE MASK OF RELIGIOUS TRADITIONS

that ill-timed moment. Unlike the docile, innocent, and ignorant bovines feeding in fields around the world, these particular bulls have been trained to be ferocious, belligerent, and blood-thirsty beasts—or so they say.

People from many nations have called for the end of this spectacle, citing the serious injuries and deaths that have resulted. They overlook the deep roots of this event in the cultural heritage of a nation. Although there is nothing inherently wrong with the animals or even the human participants in such an event, has its tradition outlived its useful purpose?

People tend to gravitate toward polar extremes. Once we discover that there is a potential for harm in something, we tend to want to ban it entirely. It is not without reason that someone came up with the cliché, "Don't throw the baby out with the bathwater!" On the other hand, people get so settled in their ruts that they ignore the better way.

Many times in our mission to destroy sacred cows, we create a self-righteous ranch full of a brand-new breed of the same. Yeah, you might want to read that sentence again.

As a young boy growing up on a small farm, I learned that hybrids of any species, plant or animal, are hardier than purebreds. What we need are some Cross-bred institutions that take advantage of the best of what tradition has preserved for us, enhanced and balanced by the best of cutting-edge innovative thinking—fueled by the Holy Spirit.

Mad Is Bad

As you read previously, in recent years, "mad cow disease" has caused considerable alarm around the world. In 1996, following outbreaks of the disease among British cattle, the

British government took a number of steps, including the slaughtering of all cattle believed to be infected. This whole-sale slaughter of all the potentially infected animals was the only apparent solution available to the authorities. Many of us will long remember the vivid television news images of mountains of cows being incinerated.

Many, in fact most, of these cows were not infected. But in order to protect the public, the only option was to completely destroy these herds. What a shame that so many useful animals, along with the businesses of their owners, went up in smoke.

More recently, tests have been devised to better detect infection in individual animals so they can be quarantined and destroyed without having to resort to the destruction of entire herds.

As described in earlier chapters, sacred cows can be menaces to the Kingdom of God, and should be destroyed. No doubt, "mad" is "bad," but are all cows mad? When our approach is the wholesale eradication of all tradition, many useful institutions will perish unnecessarily in the process. The baby will get thrown out with the bathwater!

How much better it is to *"prove all things; hold fast that which is good"* (1 Thess. 5:21).

Tradition is not a dirty word. Traditions come into existence simply because we discover good solutions to recurring problems and maintain these solutions over a period of time.

It is only when we serve the tradition, instead of the tradition serving our needs, that we run into trouble.

The cows of the Bible provide a perfect example.

King Solomon was privileged to build an edifice that many scholars feel should have been numbered with the "Seven

Wonders of the Ancient World." Solomon's father, David, had spent years collecting the materials for the construction of a Temple for Yahweh, though he himself was not allowed by God to build it. The Books of First Kings (chapters 5–8) and Second Chronicles (chapters 2–7) describe this lavish building in intricate detail.

According to the Septuagint and Syriac manuscripts, the portico or porch at the front of the Temple was almost 35 feet wide and well over 200 feet high. That's a 20-story high building![1]

The Temple was built of great stones, huge cedar beams, and boards overlaid with gold. Its value by today's standards has been estimated between $2 and $5 billion, and was no doubt the most costly and resplendent building on earth at the time. It was built after the general plan of the older Tabernacle, except everything was double in size.

But as we study the description of this fantastic structure and its appointments, something strange arrests our attention. In spite of the fact that the Third Commandment explicitly states, *"Thou shalt not make unto thee any graven image, or any likeness of any thing that is in heaven above, or that is in the earth beneath, or that is in the water under the earth,"* (Exod. 20:4) and in spite of the fact that the original Tabernacle contained no such images, in Solomon's Temple we find a number of suspicious creatures. (See First Kings 5–7.)

Solomon hired a Tyrian to take charge of the work and used Phoenician craftsmen, so it is not surprising to find parallels to the design of the Temple and its decoration in surviving examples of Phoenician or Canaanite handiwork. In Solomon's Temple we find such things as "carved figures of cherubim...and open flowers," "lily work in the porch," "pomegranates," "lions, and palm trees."

The most startling scene is the huge water basin that loomed just outside the porch. This ceremonial washing basin was made of cast metal, circular in shape, and measured over 17 feet from rim to rim and stood almost 9 feet high. Its circumference was 52 feet and the metal was as thick as a man's hand, about 4 inches thick. It has been estimated to have weighed as much as 30 tons and to have held up to 20,000 gallons of water.

Can you guess what would support such a huge basin? Twelve bronze bulls—three facing north, three facing west, three facing south, and three facing east. Their hindquarters were toward the center and the basin rested on top of their backs.

What are these graven images doing in such sacred surroundings? Did Solomon commit the same evil as did Aaron before him and Jeroboam just a generation later? Is there a way to justify this seemingly flagrant violation of the Third Commandment?

Many scholars are of the opinion that Solomon did indeed make a grievous mistake by installing these bulls on this most holy site, and that this action was but a prelude to his later, much more prolific idolatrous practices, when he married many heathen women and allowed them to import their religions into Israel.

But we cannot disregard the fact that upon the completion and dedication of this marvelous structure, God Himself honored the work of Solomon by descending in a Shekinah cloud and filling the Temple with His presence.

It came even to pass, as the trumpeters and singers were as one, to make one sound to be heard in praising and thanking the Lord; and when they lifted up

their voice with the trumpets and cymbals and instru-
ments of music, and praised the Lord, saying, For He
is good; for His mercy endureth for ever: that then the
house was filled with a cloud, even the house of the
Lord; so that the priests could not stand to minister by
reason of the cloud: for the glory of the Lord had filled
the house of God (2 Chronicles 5:13-14).

Surely if God had objected to the presence of those bulls in the inner court, He would not have shown up and graced the building with His glory! Having already demonstrated how vehemently He could respond with displeasure when He killed Uzzah for simply reaching out to steady the Ark to keep it from toppling, surely if He had been displeased with Solomon's actions, He would have communicated that displeasure in some adverse way. But instead He validated the entirety of the construction, including the 12 bronze bulls, by personally manifesting His presence in a visible and magnificent way.

So how can we reconcile God's acceptance of Solomon's bronze bulls with God's rejection of Aaron's golden calf at Sinai and Jeroboam's two golden calves at Bethel and Dan? Why were Solomon's cows "OK"?

This question can be answered in at least four ways. Solomon's cows were OK because of the:

- Attitude and declaration accompanying Solomon's bulls.

- Position that Solomon's bulls occupied.

- Number and orientation of Solomon's bulls.

- Subsequent history of Solomon's bulls.

Platitudes and Attitudes

First, we see that Solomon's bulls were OK when we consider the *attitude* and *declarations* of the three men associated with these cows.

At Sinai, Aaron had declared, *"These be thy gods, O Israel, which brought thee up out of the land of Egypt"* (Exod. 32:4b).

At Bethel and Dan, Jeroboam had declared, *"Behold thy gods, O Israel, which brought thee up out of the land of Egypt"* (1 Kings 12:28).

But in Jerusalem, at the dedication of the Temple, Solomon declared: *"O Lord God of Israel, there is no God like Thee in the heaven, nor in the earth; which keepest covenant, and showest mercy unto Thy servants."* He went on to say in that same prayer: *"But will God in very deed dwell with men on the earth? behold, heaven and the heaven of heavens cannot contain Thee; how much less this house which I have built!"* (2 Chron. 6:14a,18).

The difference is not in the *platitudes,* but in the *attitudes!*

The word *platitude* comes from the French "plat" which means flat and from which we get our English word "plate." A platitude is basically a dull or trite remark, especially one uttered as if it were fresh or profound. Like a plate, it has a broad surface, but no depth. A platitude is a *conjecture* of the lips, but an attitude is a *confession* of the heart. (So remember, guys—the next time you have a domestic quarrel in the kitchen and you witness a flying saucer as it whirls past your head—it's only a platitude, not an attitude!)

Solomon's prayer was certainly not a platitude. It was a petition that resounded from an attitude of reverent humility and genuine worship. Aaron's and Jeroboam's platitudes exemplified the selfish exploitation of religion. Solomon's heart was to please the Lord; Aaron and Jeroboam sought to appease the people. Solomon did not set his 12 bronze bulls up as gods to be worshiped; in contrast, Aaron and Jeroboam were guilty of flagrant idolatry.

Service, Not Supremacy

Second, we see that Solomon's bulls were OK when we note the *position* Solomon's bulls occupied. They were under the basin, bearing the load. Could it be that Solomon made the images of oxen to support this great cistern in contempt of the golden calf that Israel had worshiped? Just maybe he wanted the people to see there was nothing worthy of adoration in these colossal figurines; they were designed and built to be *support posts*, not *sacred potentates*.

When the cows in our lives are kept in their proper role of *service*, and not allowed to ascend to an inappropriate position of *supremacy*, then we have nothing to worry about as far as sacred cows are concerned.

Foreshadows of the Future

Third, we see that Solomon's bulls were OK when we note the *number* of bulls Solomon used—12, the number of the tribes of Israel; and their *orientation*, facing the four points of the compass. At the same time we should remember that the purpose of the basin was the ceremonial cleansing of the priests prior to their duty in the sacred confines of the sanctuary. Solomon's symbolism could not have been accidental. This was an obvious allusion to the fact that God's original intent for the whole of Israel—all the tribes, not just the

Levites—was to be a nation of priests, all of whom were to serve as a conduit of blessing to all the other nations of the earth. Their role of service was to take the glory of God to the ends of the earth—north, east, south, and west.

When God gathered his people at Sinai, His intent was to consecrate the entire population as a nation of priests. He only resorted to sanctifying the Levites as the priestly tribe after the leaders of Israel, frightened by the fire and thunder on the mountain, refused to meet with God face to face. The people essentially placed themselves in a position of needing a priesthood rather than *being* a priesthood. Thank God today we have a new will and testament!

God never abandoned His original plan. His desire was, and still is, for all His blood-bought, chosen people to be priests who serve the errant nations of the world, ministering reconciliation with their Creator. What a picture of God's grand design Solomon's bulls are! What a foreshadow of what God intends His Church to be today! Oh, if only we would capture this vision, bear up under the load of the priestly calling, point ourselves toward the four ends of the earth, and carry the glorious message of reconciliation to the world.

The original brazen laver in the wilderness Tabernacle was only a small basin. Solomon's contribution was an enormous "sea" that required the strength of bulls for its support. It cast a shadow into the future of a tremendous army, a victorious militant band of royal ambassadors invading this planet with the "word of reconciliation"! (See Second Corinthians 5:18-19.)

Aaron's calf and Jeroboam's calves were shadows of a shameful past—a longing to return to the fleshpots of Egypt. Solomon's bulls were a foreshadow of a glorious future for a people destined to reign with Christ as kings and priests in this life!

In the Kingdom, the object (God) was in place before the light. In fact, the object turned the light on, or should I say He spoke the light on. So in numerous Old Testament scenes, we can imagine what our Father plans for us as we stand in His shadow—the foreshadow of the future.

'Til the Cows Come Home

Fourth, we see that Solomon's bulls were OK when we observe the subsequent *history* of the presence of these bulls in the Temple. We see that there is a definite correlation between the presence of these support animals and the spiritual status of God's people at the time.

Solomon's bronze bulls did not remain perpetually in the Temple. They were later removed from the Temple courts, not because someone objected to them on the grounds of any supposed idol worship, but rather they were removed by King Ahaz in order to make room for the pagan worship of the Assyrians. The entire story is found in Second Kings chapters 16–17, and has its own lessons and applications that are beyond the scope of this writing. However, the story's relevance to our contrast between OK cows and sacred cows is clearly seen in the fact that immediately after the removal of Solomon's twelve bronze bulls, two idols in the shape of calves were erected. One has to wonder where these idols came from.

Later, King Ahaz' son, Hezekiah, brought a revival to Judah and destroyed all the pagan altars and other idolatrous trappings that Ahaz had installed throughout Jerusalem. Furthermore, he re-sanctified and re-installed all of the sacred Temple objects that Ahaz had removed—including Solomon's 12 bronze bulls. The fact that Hezekiah felt these articles needed to be sanctified anew leads one to wonder if they were not used as idols by the wicked King Ahaz and his cohorts.

The 12 bronze bulls remained in the Temple courts until they were finally carted away by Nebuchadnezzar when he destroyed Jerusalem and the Temple in 586 B.C. Of course the valuable contents of the Temple had been plundered many times through the years by foreign invaders as well as Judah's own kings; but it is interesting to note that the last things to go were the bronze bulls—the burden-bearers—the servants.

The message is crystal-clear: Sacred cows make their appearance when institutions of service are removed from their divinely ordained place of submission and elevated to positions of preeminence.

There is a direct correlation in the subsequent history of Solomon's bulls between the spiritual state of the covenant people and the presence of the bulls in the Temple.

- Solomon installed the bulls in the Temple as burden-bearers, and the glory of God filled the Temple.

- Ahaz removed the bulls in deference to a pagan enemy, and the nation fell into wholesale idolatry.

- Hezekiah reinstalled the bulls to their rightful place and position, and the nation experienced revival.

- Finally, when the nation became repeatedly and fatally mired in idolatry, God sent a destroyer in the person of Nebuchadnezzar who removed the bulls for the final time and wrecked the Temple. (See Jeremiah 52:17-20.)

Solomon's cows were allowed (in contrast to other cows that were rejected by God) because their function was strictly defined within the broader scope of God's redemptive purpose. Cows that fail this litmus test are sacred cows that must be shunned at all costs.

Many of our traditions are practical and functional, and we should continue them in our efforts to fulfill our roles as ambassadors of the Kingdom of God and as slaves of righteousness. Just as in the days of the divided kingdom, when the useful, serviceable cows filled their appropriate place, God is acknowledged as occupying His rightful place, and God's people can function in their appointed place.[2]

There are other traditions, however, that have served their practical usefulness and need to be discarded or, at the most, relegated to museums as antiques. Still others are outright obstacles to the advancement of the Kingdom in the earth, and should be dispassionately destroyed. They are sacred cows that need to be slaughtered in the interests of a starving world—even if they are the preacher's pet.

I have a very dear friend who is a big game hunter. When you walk into his house you feel as if you're being watched by all these "dead and stuffed" animals, but there is never a concern that they could harm you. They are trophies of a hunt, a place and time, not live animals anymore—only icons to jog the memory of a successful and pleasurable event.

When my friend first started collecting these furry figurines, they were relegated to what he called the trophy room. Then his wife picked up the sport, and now there are so many formaldehyde-filled exotic species they are in every room of the house—well, maybe not the kitchen! Visiting in that home really takes some getting used to, because even if you're in a room with only one person, you feel you've just joined a "small group" ministry.

Things would be much easier for modern Christianity if we had a room somewhere designated for the stuffed animals, and we kept them relegated to that room only. A place where we could differentiate: between the stuffed and the truly sacred; between the lifeless and the animated; between the past and the present; between what was a trophy of yesterday and what is a timeless treasure today. This room would serve to remind us that it's not only about what's good or bad, but about what is appropriate.

Jesus said, when confronted about His disciples' disregard for properly keeping the Sabbath:

Have ye never read what David did, when he had need, and was an hungered, he, and they that were with him? How he went into the house of God in the days of Abiathar the high priest, and did eat the showbread, which is not lawful to eat but for the priests, and gave also to them which were with him? And He said unto them, The sabbath was made for man, and not man for the sabbath: therefore the Son of man is Lord also of the sabbath (Mark 2:25-28).

I am merely stressing a point Christ has already made: when the maintenance of an institution gets in the way of the function of the Kingdom, we have missed the point and lost our way. Institutions, even those given and ordained by God Himself, are to serve God's purpose and are for humankind's good. When they get in the way of the purposes of the Kingdom and become obstacles to the well-being of the people of the Kingdom, they are no more than sacred cows.

However, when they promote the advancement of the Kingdom, even things that would, in other circumstances, be disallowed are sanctioned by God and blessed with His Shekinah presence.

Just because something does not have the right "label" does not disqualify it for service in the Kingdom.

Once when the disciple John observed, *"Master, we saw one casting out devils in Thy name; and we forbad him, because he followeth not with us," Jesus responded by saying, "Forbid him not: for he that is not against us is for us"* (Luke 9:49-50).

Our God is so incredibly practical. While we never want to lose sight of the fact that God despises the religiosity that impedes the advancement of the Kingdom, we also must never lose sight of the inclusiveness of His love and the very practical functionality that He honors. Just because somebody doesn't carry our particular denominational badge does not automatically make their practices sacred cows. Many times we oppose the traditions of others simply because we have failed to understand their purpose and function. A closer examination of the situation may reveal that their cows better serve the Kingdom than do some of our own high-bred heifers.

All of our cows don't have to die. Cows are neither good nor evil in and of themselves. They are either valid or invalid depending on their purpose and functionality. The "fatted calf" never becomes a "sacred cow" unless we religiously keep it in the pen and refuse to let it be used for its intended purpose. Cows that are OK are those whose functionality is aligned with divine purpose to serve the ends of the Kingdom. The next chapter gives insight about where your cows fall within God's divine purpose.

Endnotes

1. Other scholars dispute these measurements, believing the portico to have been only 20 cubits high (compare the translations of Second Chronicles 3:4 in the New King James Version and the New International Version).

2. See Second Corinthians 5:20.

Epigraph

The writers against religion, whilst they oppose very system, are wisely careful never to set up any of their own.

—*Edmond Burke*

I am not interested in the past. I am interested in the future, for that is where I expect to spend the rest of my life.

—*Charles F. Kettering*

It is so soon that I am done for I wonder what I was begun for.

—*Tombstone inscription*

Notes

_____

_____

_____

_____

_____

_____

_____

_____

_____

CHAPTER 8

Cow Testing

"Searching for God's DNA"

AS we conclude our time together, I don't want to just point a finger at all the things we're doing wrong without providing a hand to make them right. This book is certainly not conclusive. But I hope it has stirred you to look at masks and sacred cows differently. As we continue to work in Kingdom business, we need to frequently test our systems and programs to determine if they truly are God-purposed calves and not sacred cows.

Is it possible to conduct such a test? Is there an easy way to detect the difference between a device that's become a sacred cow and one whose core is the Saving Lamb? Can we know for sure what is behind the mask?

The answer is yes to all three questions. Without developing an entire new set of manuscripts, which I may do later on this particular subject, I'll introduce to you, "Spiritual DNA Testing," a simple, user-friendly search for the DNA of God.

Every cell in every living thing has DNA, a molecule that contains all the information about that organism. Lengths of ladder-like connected DNA molecules called genes are similar to tiny pieces of a secret code. They determine the composition of an organism down to the most intricate and minute detail.

Every element about our physical makeup traveled from our parents down these magnificent DNA ladders, to give us the color of our eyes and hair, our height, and even our width. However, our width is determined more by our DTE (Determination to Eat) than by our DNA! Although no two organisms (except identical twins) have the same exact DNA, the similarities between relatives are easily discovered. In fact, relatives look more alike under a microscope than they do to the naked eye. That could be a frightening thought!

In recent years the use of DNA evidence at a crime scene has been most useful. Matching a body fluid sample, speck of blood, or one single bit of hair has been the link needed to put guilty people behind bars, and set free others who were initially charged with the crime. DNA is the "bottom line" when it comes to proof positive. In other words, if your particular DNA is discovered at the crime scene, it means you had been there.

Likewise, you can examine any portion of God or His Kingdom, any cell, so to speak, and He is there. Examine a parable Christ told, a miracle He performed, His creation, or a mere gesture—God is there. In every cell you can find the DNA of God. No wonder Christ said, "When you've seen Me you've seen My father" (see John 14:9).

Man was created in the image of God. Paul says in Ephesians 2:10, "*For we are His workmanship, created in Christ Jesus unto good works, which God hath before ordained that we should walk in them.*" We are mistaken when we think God created man and then gave him a gift. I believe that God created a gift and gave to it a man.

This is the reason so many go through life unfulfilled. They are trying to live their lives using another's DNA. It's like asking a bird to fly with a lizard's tail.

Counselors make a lot of money trying to help people find and solve their problems. All the while there is no synchronization between the gift and the gifted. The frustration comes when we try to fit a gift with a human, instead of fitting the human to the gift.

We must synchronize the gift, the gifted and the gadget (cow or program). When we run everything through the DNA test, we will prevent a lot of unequal yoking with sacred cows.

Finding the DNA of God is really quite simple. The test is designed to be a compact laboratory that can be transported to the battlefield as well as the harvest field. It consists of three easy-to-answer questions. These questions must be posed to any and every system, program, device or function that the modern Christian would be tempted to use in order to be part of the master plan of God. These three questions clearly reveal evidence, one way or the other, of God's presence or the absence of it—a useful cow or a sacred cow.

Question # 1—Was It Conceived by God?

Almost every parent can share the same story of their toddler children attempting to walk around in their father's or mother's shoes. Late one evening at home after a long day, I heard my little boy say, "Look, Daddy! Look, Daddy—they fit!" I turned to see and ultimately capture one of those "parent pictures." It was the kind only a mother or father can truly see and appreciate.

There he stood with nothing on but a Pamper, a proud grin, and my old boots. The boots were so large their tops were pressing against the bottom of his diaper. The picture got more interesting as he struggled to walk. After a series of desperate attempts and several topples, he finally gave up and we both ended up rolling on the floor with laughter.

Does the fact that my boots didn't fit him mean that he may not be my own flesh and blood? Not hardly! I knew it was only a matter of time—growth and maturity. Now he wears my stuff pretty well—in fact many of my shirts and jackets have ended up in his closet!

I know he's my son, not based on whether he can wear my boots, but based on how well I know his mom. I happened to be there when he was conceived and when he was born. So I should know! A DNA test would prove me right.

This first DNA test question is very important, because it protects a lot of innocent and immature (boot wearing) programs from slaughter. What if Joseph, Jesus' earthly father, had gone with his first instinct? But

Because Joseph her husband was a righteous man and did not want to expose her to public disgrace, he had in mind to divorce her quietly. But after he had considered this, an angel of the Lord appeared to him in a dream and said, "Joseph son of David, do not be afraid to take Mary home as your wife, because what is conceived in her is from the Holy Spirit" (Matthew 1:19-20 NIV).

The big looming question Joseph had was answered. If she is pregnant, who is the father? There was only one correct answer, only one that would calm his troubled mind. *"What is conceived in her is from the Holy Spirit."*

If the ideas and programs we deal with cannot produce a birth certificate with the Father's name on it, they were probably concocted and not conceived.

Question # 2—Has It Been Adopted by God?

Apostle James wrote, *"Every good and perfect gift is from above, coming down from the Father of the heavenly lights, who does not change like shifting shadows"* (James 1:17 NIV).

I don't want to imply that our Father needs to adopt anything—He already owns it all, yes, even the cows on the hills.

> *For every animal of the forest is Mine, and the cattle on a thousand hills. I know every bird in the mountains, and the creatures of the field are Mine. If I were hungry I would not tell you, for the world is Mine, and all that is in it* (Psalm 50:10-12 NIV).

The second question is relative to the situations in our life that did not originate from God; but when all was said and done and the smoke had cleared, He adopted them and made them His own. We find a perfect example in the troubles of Joseph,:

> *"You intended to harm me, but God intended it for good to accomplish what is now being done, the saving of many lives. So then, don't be afraid. I will provide*

for you and your children." And he reassured them and spoke kindly to them. Joseph stayed in Egypt, along with all his father's family. He lived a hundred and ten years and saw the third generation of Ephraim's children. Also the children of Makir son of Manasseh were placed at birth on Joseph's knees (Genesis 50:20-23 NIV).

October 3, 2002, is a day my family and I will never forget. A category 4 hurricane had smashed into the coast of Louisiana and worked its way northward to the area where we lived. Being an adventurous person, I decided that better than just shutting in and waiting for the storm to pass, I should get out and get involved. My redheaded daughter, who is just as adventurous, decided to go along for the ride. Boy, was it ever a ride!

We jumped into my 4x4 pickup and hit the streets. After a few minutes of riding around watching trees bend, power lines sway and billboards tumble, we saw a way to be of assistance. A massive oak tree had fallen across a major thoroughfare and needed to be removed.

I gave my daughter a yellow slicker suit to wear along with explicit instructions about how to respond if a twister was seen spinning off from the hurricane. (She later laughed about which would have been worse—being swept away by the twister or drowning in the ditch where I had told her to lie down.)

After disengaging the winch on my truck, I cut a path with my machete through the huge tree branches. All the while I was looking for a good spot to tie the cable so the colossal obstruction could be moved out of the path of travelers—not that there were many. Most intelligent people were at home waiting for the storm to pass—according to the truck radio, we were literally in the eye of the storm.

There was, however, one other traveler—a drunken man who was driving 45 mph on a joy ride in pelting rain in a worn-out Pontiac. To make matters worse, he was coming straight toward me!

The car struck me somewhere around the kneecaps, cartwheeled me into the windshield, and then slammed me face down onto the pavement. At least that's what I've been told. The last thing I remember is hearing the policeman who was standing nearby call my name.

After several days in the hospital, tongue reconstruction, and months of convalescence, I am a grateful trophy of grace.

Questions: Did God plan this to happen? Was this His idea conceived in Heaven?

Not necessarily.

What I didn't realize was, at the time of the impact my daughter went to her knees in the ditch where she was standing and spoke the most powerful thing she could think of.

Jesus!

Jesus!

Somewhere between the crash and the calling of that all-powerful name, God intercepted a fiasco and turned it into favor. He might not have conceived it, but He was willing to adopt it.

Question # 3—Does It Bear the Fruit of God?

The last question in the DNA test is not last because it's the least important; in fact it is the bottom line question. The first two questions deal with opinions as to whether God conceived or adopted something—the age-old argument about what God causes and allows. But this final question is the part of the cow test that is infallible.

When I ask, "Does it bear the fruit of God?" I'm also asking "Does it have the DNA of God?" What is the fruit and DNA of God? I believe they are one and the same.

The *fruit* of the spirit is the *DNA* of God!

> *But the fruit of the Spirit is love, joy, peace, patience, kindness, goodness, faithfulness, gentleness and self-control. Against such things there is no law. Those who belong to Christ Jesus have crucified the sinful nature with its passions and desires. Since we live by the Spirit, let us keep in step with the Spirit* (Galatians 5:22-25 NIV).

In previous verses Paul mentions, "*...the works of the flesh are manifest, which are these; Adultery, fornication, uncleanness...*" (Gal. 5:19). In reference to the flesh he calls the attributes "works," but when he mentions the Spirit, he alludes to a tree of fruit bearing nine luscious varieties. Fruit is the natural outcropping of the Holy Spirit within us.

It's noteworthy that Paul enumerates 17 "*works of the flesh*" and only nine manifestations of "*the fruit of the Spirit.*"[1] This is a perfect illustration of how quickly we can build numerous sacred cows when we are absent of divinity.

On the other hand, when we are infused with the wonderful and perfect DNA of God, the effect is a natural fruit-bearing process. He is the vine, we are the branches. The end result is much fruit. What a wonderful family tree!

Every program, system, sermon, device—and even the annual church picnic—should be fruit checked. Each must be either assisting in producing the fruit of the Spirit or driven and motivated by the fruit of the Spirit.

Anything that cannot trace its genetics back to the Father is a sacred cow and must be destroyed. So go ahead, look behind the mask, grab the bull by the horns, and let's have a barbeque!

Udderly—the end.

Disclaimer: No live animals were harmed during the production of this book.

Endnote

1. *Jamieson, Fausset, and Brown Commentary*, Electronic Database, 1997 by Biblesoft.

Notes

_____

_____

_____

_____

_____

_____

_____

_____

_____

_____

Ministry Contacts

Mark Briggs Ministries International

Taking people to the next level through inspiration,
information and impartation.

Riverpark Church

An in-the-Bible, out-of-the-box church,
presenting the life of Christ in a new way.

Global Samaritan

Providing humanitarian relief
in times of crisis at home and abroad.

Contact information:

P.O. Box 5608
Shreveport, LA 71135
Telephone: 318-865-1110
Fax: 318-865-1454

E-mail: pastor@riverparkchurch.net
Internet: www.markbriggs.org
http://www.riverparkchurch.net
www.riverparkchurch.net

Tom Winters, Attorney/Literary Agent
Winters, King & Associates, Inc.
Tulsa, OK

Additional copies of this book and other
book titles from DESTINY IMAGE are
available at your local bookstore.

Call toll free: 1-800-722-6774.

Send a request for a catalog to:

Destiny Image₍ₐ₎ Publishers, Inc.
P.O. Box 310
Shippensburg, PA 17257-0310

*"Speaking to the Purposes of God for this
Generation and for the Generations to Come."*

**For a complete list of our titles,
visit us at www.destinyimage.com**

1 John 5:14-15